Heartbreak Kids

Heartbreak Kids

—

A Survival Guide for Parents

Jeri Schweigler, EdD

ISBN-13: 9781530024513
ISBN-10: 153002451X

My thanks to Ron Arkin for validating the importance of this subject and to both Roger Shantz and Mimi Jensen for editing and encouraging.

Table of Contents

Preface

THIS BOOK IS not about parenting skills, nor is it specifically about children. It does not directly address strategies to effectively deal with troubled children. This book is about the heartbreak of parenting children who are not thriving, or whose situations or behaviors create heartbreak for parents. I call this book a survival guide for parents as it addresses the tools and perspective needed to alleviate the damaging effects of prolonged stress created by heartbreaking parental situations.

The premise of this book is that there is only one type of relationship that is truly unconditional: the relationship between parent and child. Love, concern, and caring for our children do not alter as conditions or situations change. However, distress, anxiety and fear escalate and accumulate in the body and brain when a parent cannot find a clear path to the well-being of their child.

We may think of our love relationships and our friendships as unconditional. We speak of unconditional love in the words and lyrics of poetry and music. Literature abounds with the promise of love that has no conditions. "I'll love you until the rivers all run dry" and no matter what you say or do. However, as conditions change, love is altered. Unconditional love is reserved for parent and child.

I worked with a 78- year old woman who had recently lost her beloved husband and father of their three children. Her grief was immense. She had lost her best friend, her lover, her life partner. She had lost the person that "made my life meaningful." Caring for him during the short time he lived after his heart attack made her feel even closer.

As she finally brought herself to the dreaded task of sorting through his personal possessions, she discovered a box containing cards and letters from a woman with whom he had been having an affair for 20 years. Did this 'condition' change her love? YES and replaced it with confusion, abandonment, anger, shame, humiliation, disbelief, and a whole different kind of grief.

A middle aged female patient, Laura, was dealing with her adult schizophrenic son, Ben. Because of his refusal to comply with his medication schedule, his heavy drinking, and a subtle threat of violence, Laura refused to have him come to her house unless he agreed to take medication and abstain from drinking. He continued to act out, sitting on her front porch begging to spend the night. He continued to use alcohol and refused medication. She had him arrested several times, but law enforcement could not help him.

Did this 'condition' change her love for him? NO in the sense that her daily worry about his physical and mental health, her guilt, shame, empathy, sadness and grief remained constant. "I feel guilty if I buy myself something expensive thinking he is probably living on the street." The empathic connection had not altered. Each time he was arrested, she visited him and spent the rest of the day in tears. Hope, expectation, pride, joy had long ago faded, but love had not diminished. It is the 'tie that binds' forever.

This book addresses parents who have the capacity for healthy attachment to their children, have devoted immense emotional and physical energy to their children's situations and experience agony and heartbreak watching them suffer and struggle coping with life, for a multitude of reasons. These struggles may be due to mental or physical illness, to personality, behavioral or attitudinal issues, to neurological or development disorders, or to addictions. Whatever the cause, the resulting struggles consume parents with prolonged and immobilizing stress.

This book is intended to empower parents whose lives are wrapped around the quest to assist their struggling children toward healthy, independent lives and whose greatest fear is that this will not be possible. How can parents, consumed with worry and anxiety and drained of time and energy, focus attention on their own goals, emotional needs, relationships, and physical well-being? To parents who are deeply entrenched in their children's struggles, believing this question to be relevant and important is difficult.

For some, the answer seems binary: total devotion to the need of the child (including adult children) or turn away. A patient's husband left her six months after their son was born with Down syndrome. He could not endure the prospect of losing the life he had. He could not envision a life of his own if he stayed to raise their son together. So he turned away.

A 55- year old patient, still engrossed in trying to find a way to motivate her 24 year old son to leave his bedroom, and her house, long enough to get a job or enroll in school, 'suddenly' realized that she needed to find a way to focus time and attention on her physical fitness and make use of her talent for running non-profit businesses. It took the grim results of blood tests to bring her to that 'sudden' realization. All lab reports suggested an urgency to reverse the effects of neglect to her body, stress she had internalized, and exhaustion from worry and anxiety. If she did not find a way to focus on herself, there might not be anything left to give.

The chapters in this book are for those who have attended lovingly and effectively to children who break their hearts. These children are heartbreakers because they are so loved. Nothing breaks our hearts more than the pain of our children's struggles or our struggles with our children. All healthy parents endure a degree of that pain alongside their children. However, those heartbreaks usually come in smaller doses: academic struggles, anxiety and fears, difficulty making friends. For the most part, we have reason to believe these experiences will pass and our children will learn and grow through them. In fact, these life pains are important developmental learning experiences. They are life's classroom. These children keep moving forward. They thrive.

I use the word "non-thriving" throughout the book. Its use is intended to be a generic, catch-all for the many sources of heartbreak endured by a parent. Obviously, these children need help and resources but so do the parents if they are to create their own treatment plans. It is for those loving and struggling parents that this book is written.

CHAPTER 1

The Heartbreak

A DEEPLY FELT pain throughout the body, an aching empathy activated by dread, fear, disappointment, and lack of control. This is heartbreak: the crushing sorrow parents experience while watching someone they love suffer from an inability or a refusal to thrive. The object of that sorrow is their child, the person with whom they most likely have the strongest empathic connection. They cannot experience the suffering and struggle of their child without experiencing heartbreak and its many accompanying emotional and physiological side effects.

In my work as a psychotherapist, I have not seen greater heartbreak than that of parents who are experiencing their child, regardless of the age or reason, as unable or unwilling to thrive. Parents need assurance that their child will move forward through developmental stages onto a path that offers the possibility of health and happiness. The absence of that assurance leaves parents to experience the all-consuming emotional and physiological symptoms of stress.

General Adaptation Syndrome

Heartbreak encompasses helplessness, dread, anticipatory anxiety and catastrophic expectations that signal our bodies to turn on the stress response, affecting our emotions, thoughts, and physiological processes. Hans Selye, an Australian endocrinologist, conducted ground breaking research that identified a stress model based on what he labeled the general adaptation syndrome. He postulated that stress is a major cause of disease because chronic

1

stress causes long-term chemical changes. "Every stress leaves an indelible scar and the organism pays for its survival after a stressful situation by becoming a little older." (Selye 1976)

Selye is known as the father of stress research because his work identified the role stress plays in disease. He described three stages of response to stress: alarm, resistance, and exhaustion. The first stage we know about. For parents, it is anything that signals a serious concern regarding the well-being of their child, no matter how old that child may be. Parents who have experienced multiple or continuous difficulties or worries about their children develop fine-tuned antennas for danger.

A patient, Jane, has an adult daughter now in her fourth rehabilitation program for drug abuse. Every call from her daughter can signal either relief or "a sickening feeling in my stomach" that something is not right. Will she complete the program? Will she leave against therapeutic advice and return to her drug using boyfriend? Jane's body and brain are on alert.

The second stage of the general adaption syndrome, resistance, is the body/brain capacity to adapt and accommodate stress. This amazingly effective mechanism is adaptive when stress is short-lived and the body and brain can return to a relaxed and restorative state. Selye wrote about resistance as the quality that permits a person to recover quickly and thrive in spite of adversity.

Thrive in spite of adversity. Not so easy to do when that adversity is dread of my child's future or my future with my child. That is the question that so many parents have: how to navigate through the tremendous emotional alarms set off by that crushing sorrow of heartbreak. With chronic stressors such as heartbreaking situations with children, the alarms do not turn off. A parent may be one phone call, one interaction, one disappointment away from alarm.

This is the stage of exhaustion that any parent, consumed by the continuous stressors of heartbreak parenting situations, knows about. It happens when the stressor continues beyond the body/brain capacity to accommodate, increasing the risk of chronic pain, health issues, disease and emotional disorders such as depression and anxiety. It is why I hear from my patients, "I feel done." "Sometimes I just want to disappear and leave this to someone else to deal with." "I feel like running away." "I don't think this will ever end."

The most recent phrase that seemed to describe what Selye was identifying in his third stage was "I'm exhausted with parenting." I heard this from a mother still addressing the lack of motivation and emotional strength in her three children, 19, 21, and 24, who were living at home. When we cannot turn off the stress response, because the alarm is continuously sounded, the body/brain becomes exhausted and the adaptive stress mechanism not only becomes ineffective but becomes harmful to health and well-being. This subject will be explored in further chapters.

Maria Lin, a parent of a special needs child, boldly identifies 5 things to know about being a special needs parent: (Huffington Report, 7/17/13)

1. I am tired.
   She is not referring to being tired of the child, but exhausted dealing with the same issues over and over with no sense of progress or solution.
2. I am jealous.
   Jealous because listening to other parents talk about the milestones and accomplishments of their children is painful (and it feels wrong somehow to be jealous.)
3. I am alone.
   A parent can feel very alone because others have a hard time understanding the pain of their situation. It can seem easier to isolate and avoid talking to people who don't understand.

4. I am scared.

    Parents are scared of the forecast for their child's future.

5. I am human.

    Human in the sense that we all have a breaking point.

This breaking point for parents of non-thriving children must be acknowledged with vigilance. Recognizing the necessity to focus on self-needs does NOT imply a neglect of the child's needs. It emphasizes, instead, a need for parents to focus on their own emotional and physical survival. Surprising to the consumed parent, attention on self needs only serves to increase their potential effectiveness as parents.

Recently a patient, Sharon, struggling with verbal abuse from both her sons, related a most disturbing scenario. Her sons accused her consistently of being a "cheap and selfish person" that caused the pending divorce between her and their father. They relentlessly called her greedy for not paying more money for their needs. She had exhaustingly attempted to defend herself by showing them court orders and emails to clarify her situation but to no avail.

In a recent verbally abusive interaction with one of her sons, she went to the garage and brought a gun into the house, setting it on the kitchen table and pleaded to her son in a state of sobbing hysteria, "Just finish me off, I can't stand it anymore." Her son, somewhat indifferently, took interest only in examining the gun with curiosity. The next morning she was distraught, embarrassed, and realized she had just given her sons more to "tell their father about."

Obviously, her approach to this situation which she "never could have imagined would happen" was not working. She was emotionally exhausted, well past a breaking point. She was trapped in a reactive emotional loop. She needed to find a way to break away from the mindset that interfered with her capacity to live her own life AND build a capacity to tolerate the emotional pain of her situation with her sons.

Another patient, Claudia, seconds after she sat down for her first session with me, burst into tears and stated "I guess I've been saving this up." For over five years she had been dealing with her daughter Teresa's addiction. Her daughter left their home at 18 to live with an uncle in Tennessee but was soon asked to leave because of her refusal to stay clean and sober. Claudia woke every morning with a pain in her chest, worried about her daughter's present and future fate. This worry was exacerbated by guilt and self-blame, even though she had done everything she could possibly do to help her daughter. Her worry was affecting her relationships and her work. She was exhausted.

The Stress Response

If we do not know how to adjust or turn off the stress response, we subject ourselves to conditions that jeopardize our health and certainly our emotional well-being. For instance, excess production of cortisol and adrenalin, two of the body's stress hormones, can cause damage to cells and muscle tissues which can become precursors to an array of disease processes such as cardiovascular conditions, stroke, gastric ulcers, and high blood sugar levels.

The alarm sets the body up to deal with a stressor. This is one of the amazing, brilliant mechanisms of the body. Blood pressure rises, more blood goes into the brain for clarity, adrenalin provides energy and we are prepared to resolve the stressor. Robert Sapolsky in his book *Why Zebras Don't Get Ulcers* (Sapolsky, 1994a) describes the natural stress response of zebras being chased by lions. The zebra's natural stress response is activated as he sprints across the savanna to escape the lion. If he succeeds, if he runs fast enough to escape the lion, the alarm turns off and the relaxation response returns. But how long could that zebra just keep running without giving in to exhaustion and capitulation? Not forever.

The most vulnerable section of the brain to be affected by this kind of chronic stress, the kind we are unable to turn off, is the hippocampus. The hippocampus is responsible for, among many other functions, memory and thinking. Both memory and thinking can suffer from the lack of ability to turn off the stress response.

When humans cannot find the turn-off valve to the stress response, the stress response becomes more damaging than the stressor itself. When the threat is physical, our bodies know how to respond and, if successful, turn off the stress response. However, the stress response we cannot as easily turn off is that initiated by psychological stress. Selye stated, "It's not the stress that kills us, it is our reaction to it."

Years ago, a friend of mine was walking in the city with her husband when a thief tore her purse from her shoulder and quickly escaped in a waiting car. My friend responded by flagging down a passing motorcycle and instructing the young and daring motorcyclist to "follow that car!" The stress response perhaps enabled her to move faster and braver than she might have if her stress hormones had not been activated. When the chase ended, her stress hormone-driven body knew how to return to normal. The chase was over. No damage done to the body or brain.

In fact, that is the brilliance of our physiological response to stress; it turns on when we need it and turns off when we don't. The stress response we cannot seem to turn off without struggle is that initiated by anxiety, worry, dread, fear, catastrophic expectations, unpredictability and lack of control. These are all emotional states that are quite familiar to the parent of a non-thriving child.

Building Resilience

So, how do we build resilience in the face of crushing sorrow? How do we find a safe harbor from the psychologically driven stress response? How do we gather at least some small kernels of empowerment while enmeshed in a backdrop of such despair? The stress response continues because all efforts to resolve or mitigate an intensely difficult family situation are ineffective in bringing about change and the stressors continue.

Much human suffering is related to the losses we experience in life. The heartbreak situations that I am addressing encompass the greatest of losses—our dreams for the future of our children and our future *with* our children. This loss is both present and future oriented. Where will he live if he can't get a job? What will happen if she has no health insurance? Who will take care of him when we die? How can I have peace of mind when she is unable or unwilling to be independent? How can I bear to hear about her loneliness? How can I get him out of the basement? How can I have any effect on her at all when her sleep cycle is reversed? Will I ever have the relationship I wanted with my child?

These parents cannot afford to let sorrow, fear, or anger break their hearts. They need to survive, need to have joy, supportive relationships, meaningful endeavors, and hope along with acceptance. There are situations where the on-going, chronic condition or behavior of a child, no matter what age, drains so much from the parent that the above sentence would seem impossible or even naïve. Heartbreak is immobilizing: shutting us down, draining energy and resources. So what resources are available to mobilize, replenish energy, and head us in a direction of acceptance and hope?

Several factors influence the psychological, emotional and behavioral responses that we have to stress:

- The cognitive interpretation we make to determine if an event is threatening or non-threatening
- The level of differentiation we have between ourselves and the stressor

- Life-style choices made when faced with the stress of heartbreak
- The degree of internal vs. external locus of control
- The level of interpersonal, social affiliation with like-minded or empathic people
- Acceptance and self-care

Cognitive Interpretations

A patient in my practice, Barbara, has a daughter, Lindsay, who at 23 cannot be motivated to do anything that moves her beyond the front door. This daughter was adopted at age 6 and has demonstrated difficult emotional, psychological and social adjustment throughout the years. Often when there was promise that something would move forward, an interview for volunteer work or an appointment with a therapist, Lindsay would reverse her sleep cycle, staying awake all night and sleeping during the day, and, therefore, renege on her commitment. On those occasions, Barbara not only felt crushed but also guilty. Her own mother had repeatedly told her before she was married that she would be a "dangerous" mother and "thank God you don't have kids."

Barbara responded to her daughter's non-thriving behavior with understandable disappointment but also with guilt instilled many years ago by a narcissistic mother. Her early childhood experiences influenced her interpretation and response to Lindsay's behavior. At times, Barbara felt that her mother must have been right and that she indeed was not a good parent. However, she was an attentive, loving parent who chose to stay home and raise her children rather than pursue her law career after graduating from Stanford. This emotional and cognitive interpretation of her situation with Lindsay served only to exacerbate her suffering and interfere with boundary setting.

Differentiation

Our children certainly feel like extensions of ourselves in many ways but, as we well know as parents, they are their own people and experience life through different lenses. If our children's struggles become internalized within ourselves, our ability to live outside their realities is diminished. If their behaviors and experiences create such guilt, hopelessness, or anxiety in us, our ability to feel in control, take action, and develop strategies are also diminished. We can deeply care, deeply empathize, and even deeply worry and still keep a breathing space between their behaviors or sufferings and our internal world.

For example, a patient of mine is consumed with sadness and worry that her child is being left out socially. This was an experience she had in her early childhood and feels that same pain as she watches her son in certain social situations. Her son, however, sees himself as happy and "quiet and serious" rather than left out. She has come to own her own unresolved pain, that has extended into her adult relationships, and therefore more effective at differentiating between what is his and what is hers. By differentiating, she can more accurately assess his development unencumbered by her own emotional responses. Perhaps, as she keeps her eye on his development, there will be something to act on, but not now. For now, she can breathe.

Interestingly, the word differentiation is defined in many ways, ranging from separation and demarcation to isolation. Its antonym is defined as unity. None of these definitions describe the psychological characteristic of differentiation and its opposite would not be unity. Differentiation is the capacity to attune to another person, to bear the pain of their sorrow or distress, their problematic behavior, their helpless/hopeless position toward life, and so many other difficult, heartbreaking scenarios, AND, at the same time, stay aware of and attuned to the state of our own emotional and physical being. We must, to some degree, see ourselves as separate in order to stay present with the pain of our children or with children who cause us pain. The goal is to create just a space between their experiences and ours, which helps parents pause and respond receptively rather than reactively. We need that space. We need that ability to pause. Differentiation will be discussed further in later chapters.

Lifestyle Choices

Barbara's personal behavioral choices are influenced by her disappointment, frustration and guilt. For her, overeating and neglect of her physical health have created or exacerbated cardiovascular issues and depression. And then, the terrible cycle begins. Her physiological and emotional issues influence her inability to turn off the stress response (the prolonged exposure to stress hormones), *AND*, her inability to turn off the stress response influences her physiological and emotional well-being. A downward spiral is created that becomes difficult to turn around.

Metabolic imbalances that lead to obesity, diabetes and other life- threatening conditions can increase vulnerability to stress. And, dealing with stress by making unhealthy lifestyle choices involving such factors as diet, level of exercise, isolation, nicotine and alcohol intake, as well as a multitude of other harmful lifestyle choices, can increase vulnerability to metabolic imbalances. How we deal with stress behaviorally and our cognitive interpretation of stressful situations influences the downward spiral of helplessness.

Barbara believed that her child's difficulty in thriving was influenced by her own "failure as a parent." She coped with the pain of this by overeating and neglecting exercise. This only prolonged and escalated her stress. She had no protective breathing space between her and her child's situation. Her life was consumed by the intense stressors.

For Barbara, her coping mechanisms, as a response to the stress of her daughter's situation, have promoted a disease process. Her stress response is not countered by a relaxation response. The two primary stress mediators, glucocorticoids, that release cortisol during stress, and catecholamines, that release adrenalin during stress, are essential processes for adaptation. They provide the body with the ability to promote conversion of protein and lipids to usable carbohydrates which serves the body well in the short run by replacing energy reserves after running away from danger. This process, however, is not useful and in fact it is harmful to the body when we are inactive (nothing we can run away from.) It can lead to increased insulin levels and can promote atherosclerotic plaque in coronary arteries. (Science, 2004)

Locus of Control

The concept of locus of control, developed by Julian Rotter in 1954, refers to the degree to which individuals believe they have direct influence on the events in their lives. An individual with high internal locus of control holds the belief that he or she has influence on the outcome of events in life including stressful situations. In contrast, a person with a high external locus of control holds the belief that the outcome of situations presented in his or her life depends more heavily on external factors.

In his book *A Season in Hell,* Percy Knauth (Knauth, 1975) describes how his prolonged sense of helplessness led to even deeper despair during an extensive period of depression.

"---a sense of hopelessness enveloped me. I knew that nothing
I did could change this situation. There was nothing I could do.

I was convinced that I was laboring under some kind of curse so that
any efforts of my own to fight the situation were foredoomed to failure"

Helplessness and shame about being helpless can compound the experience of emotional instability. Locus of control as a personality concept is simply a measure of an individual's sense of influence or lack of influence on that individual's environment.

A study most relevant to locus of control was conducted by British researchers on the effect of providing postoperative hospital patients the ability to determine when and how much medication they needed throughout the day by giving them access to a button that would dispense medication when they felt they needed it. To the surprise of many medical professionals, patients did not over medicate, did not call a nurse as much, and had lowered stress responses. Patients who could self-medicate by pushing a button to administer a dosage had far less uncertainty and knew they were in charge. This sense of control decreased their stress. (White and Pearce, 1979)

A different British study examining how a person's rank in business affected stress levels (Bredar, 2008a) showed correlation between rank at work and the degree of stress and depression an individual experienced. Those of lesser rank, and who were treated as lesser, showed more deleterious effects of stress and depression. However, those of lesser rank who found something to take control over, something that helped them feel empowered even though the stressful situation remained the same, could reverse the physiological and emotional effects of stress.

For example, a low ranking employee became the captain of the work baseball team. Finding a place and a function where he had some control and could make a contribution had favorable influence on factors like perceived stress, days of sick time, and a sense of optimism. Nothing had changed about his work situation but he had gained a sense of control and thus had lowered his stress level.

The orientation of an individual's locus of control, internal vs. external, is not a simple 'one is better to have than the other' distinction. For instance, a person with a high external locus of control (the belief that situations are influenced mostly by external factors) could be more relaxed, less driven and more content given the perception that control is external. However, a higher internal locus of control (the belief that the person has direct influence on the events in life) provides an individual with an increased sense of empowerment to master stressful events: "It is within me to make a difference in this situation." The more we believe we can have direct effect on our life circumstances, the less vulnerable and helpless we tend to feel in stressful circumstances. This does not imply that we can change the situation but we can change our perspective and response to a distressful situation.

How does any individual increase a sense of empowerment? It is empowering to take control of any aspect of life where we can affect change, regardless of how small that aspect may be. For instance, I often encourage my patients to exercise, not for weight loss, and not even for overall physical health benefits (although both are an added plus.) Unless physically impossible, taking control of exercise is something most people can do if they choose to. Change can be created, and that ability to affect change will decrease helplessness even if it is ever so slightly. And, ever so slightly counts.

Admiral William McRaven, a Navy SEAL for 36 years and a commander of the forces that killed Osama bin Laden, was invited to give the commencement speech at the University of Texas for the class of 2014. His speech focused on how to change the world. Admiral McRaven narrowed that rather encompassing topic down to ten lessons for life he learned as a Navy SEAL.

The first, and the one most relevant to our topic, was "Make your Bed." Each morning in Navy Seal training, candidates must impeccably make their beds for inspection. This meant corners tucked just so and bedcover tight, pillow centered and extra blanket folded perfectly and placed just so on the end of the bed. And, of course, the consequence of a less than perfect bed would mean blood, sweat and tears out on the beaches of San Diego.

His point? No matter what your day turns out to be, no matter how unsuccessful or dejected you might feel, you will always come home to that one thing you accomplished. And, according to Admiral McRaven, that one thing you do successfully, no matter how seemingly small or insignificant, leads you to the next task of the day, and then to the next. The lesson for the Navy SEAL candidates was that making the bed, or anything else you choose, gets you started in the right direction, and puts you in control of one area of your life. My point? Taking control of any meaningful area of your life, no matter how small, acts as a protection against the risk of learned helplessness and depression; two dangers of heartbreak parenting.

Boundary setting is another area in which an individual can take control. A patient, Renee, has been the recipient of frequent and intense abusive language from her 25-year-old, non-thriving daughter who blames and criticizes her and makes very successful attempts to pit her and her husband against each other. In Renee's attempt to stave off her daughter's abusive language and her husband's lack of support, she would avoid confronting her daughter with her responsibilities or consequences. She would also withdraw from the situation, at one time leaving for ten days to escape the interactions with her daughter.

Renee began to take control of this aspect of dealing with her daughter by acknowledging her need for her husband's support and by taking action to respond to the abusive language with consequences, boundaries and follow-through. Unfortunately her husband (wrapped up in his own fears for his daughter) was not able to support Renee's responses. Although her daughter's abusive language has reduced, her difficult attitude continues with no noticeable change.

Renee was able to feel a sense of self-validation for her own responses to her daughter and, therefore, reduce her self-doubt. As she said, "It feels so bad to want to get away from your own child." Yes, it does, AND allowing herself to be verbally abused empowered no one. She took control of that one area of her life and experienced a positive outcome.

Although this shift did not substantially change the bigger picture problem, it reduced Renee's sense of helplessness and dread. Not allowing herself to be mistreated was empowering. When dealing with heartbreak parenting, any and all sources of empowerment are of value and work toward reduction of stress. Many parents in distressful parenting situations feel disempowered and unable to gain a sense of control in, sometimes, many areas of their lives. An essential tool for struggling parents is to proactively identify where and how to take control of their own lives.

These areas of control will come in seemingly small packages: less toleration of abuse, better self-care, a contract, a plan, time away, a healthy diet, a gym schedule, support from a spouse, letting go of blame, reducing isolation, couple's therapy, individual therapy, developing and nurturing friendships, meditation and mindfulness experiences. These are all tools that an individual can use to help turn off the stress response. These areas of control are subjects addressed in later chapters.

The small packages of empowerment provide increased protection against the physiological and emotional price we pay for prolonged stress in the body. A sense of being in control of something helps develop that breathing space between a parent's internal world and the situation and behaviors of a heartbreak situation with a child.

An exercise I give to my patients is the following: Identify three areas of your life where you can take control. Write them down, along with a committed plan to implement a desirable change in each area. Make your plan specific and time-framed. Choose a person to whom you will be accountable for a timely and consistent implementation of your plan.

The "choose a person" part of this exercise is sometimes the most difficult, which takes us to the consideration of the counter-therapeutic effect of isolation in dealing with the stress of heart-break parenting. For many reasons, people under prolonged stress either over-use or under-use relationships, or they feel a need to protect themselves by isolating from relationships altogether, either to preserve energy or because of shame and embarrassment.

Supportive Relationships

> "I hear my friends talking about their college kids and how well they're doing, planning to study abroad next year and I just want to change the subject. I feel embarrassed some-times and I know I have begun to avoid some of my friends."

And another:

> "Most people I know have advice for me. They think I should be harder on him, get him out of the house. It's just too hard to explain how difficult it all is, so I don't really bring it up much."

The above quotes are from mothers who have withdrawn from once supportive relationships. There are many scenarios that lead a person to isolating behaviors. Friendships are often taxed if one person's depressive, recurrent situation permeates the bulk of all conversations. A patient Sharon is overwhelmed, to the point of physical and emotional exhaustion, with her "War of the Roses" divorce and the abusive behavior of her sons who manipulate the situation to their advantage. She cannot focus on anything else. Her life is so wrapped around the stressors that it interferes with relationships that could offer her support and distraction.

Sharon reports in her sessions with me that her friends "don't want to hear about it anymore" so she does not call them as much. I can well imagine that her friends really "don't want to hear about it anymore." However, her solution of withdrawal is not a healthy one. She has a history of emotional abandonment as a child and, of course, now is reliving the same painful experience. It was important for Sharon to reach out to these friends with understanding instead of alienation, adapting her behavior to accommodate their needs as well as hers. Cutting off relationships under stressful circumstances is an isolating and often unhealthy choice to make.

It took time for Sharon to, ever so slightly, let go of the hurt, anger, and emotional grip her situation had on her. It was important for her to find situations where people *DO* want to hear about it. She eventually found a parenting group which helped to validate her feelings about her sons and gave her options for behavioral changes to set better and stronger boundaries. Sharon's friends now get to hear about changes in her focus (a new job, a new place to live) instead of repeated stories of helplessness. She also has more emotional space to have interest in her friends' lives, although some of these friends have burned out on the years of repeated stories of helplessness.

There is, however, a very different and common scenario of isolation from friends: embarrassment and shame. A patient, Amelia, volunteers at her daughter's elementary school. Her daughter's unusual and erratic behavior, which creates negative reactions from classmates and even the teacher, is embarrassing to Amelia. She tries hard not to sign up as a volunteer when certain friends might also be volunteering. Although Amelia loves her daughter and is a fantastic parent, the embarrassment is an understandable emotion.

It was important for Amelia not to judge herself for that feeling of embarrassment so that she could work with this emotion with self-compassion and self-understanding. Avoiding friends was her attempt to protect herself from embarrassment, as well as from the guilt about being embarrassed. That behavioral choice only heightened her sense of shame. Talking to certain safe friends, surprisingly to Amelia, yielded compassion and empathy which helped turn her embarrassment from shame to acceptance. Amelia also discovered that she was not as alone in her shameful feeling of embarrassment as she thought. Although her experience with her child was perhaps more extreme than others had experienced, the feeling of embarrassment of a child's behavior was not as foreign to her friends as she would have imagined. As her shame reduced, access to supportive interactions opened to her. The embarrassment is still there but the shame is no longer a barrier to supportive relationships. Embarrassment is about a behavior, while shame is about a deep negative sense of self.

Another scenario of isolation involves an avoidant personality style. Someone who is avoidant finds a way to deal with conflict without exposing himself to emotional vulnerability. People prone to avoidance may intellectualize, distract, or focus on attending to another person rather than exposing themselves to vulnerability. This personality style usually has its origins in early childhood experiences that involve dismissive and neglectful or intrusive parents. When an avoidant person meets crisis in a relationship, they are often out of touch with feelings and pull away, unable to use relationships as support or comfort. They push forward, often in denial, unable to reach out for help. Fostering a supportive relationship is often a difficult task for an individual who has learned to avoid conflict and exposure of difficult feelings. Understanding the fear of vulnerability, and the historical good reasons for that fear, is the first step to being able to accept true support from others.

Isolation is a condition that contributes to loneliness and alienation. When our defenses against pain insulate us from connection with others, the defense itself becomes harmful. Although isolation can appear to keep us safe, it actually leaves us more vulnerable. Interpersonal connection fosters a sense of community, and we don't want to be without a community while enduring the prolonged stress of heartbreak situations. In fact, it is never a good thing to be without a community.

And the worst of isolation:

> "My husband and I can't talk about our daughter. I always feel it's them against me and I'm the bad guy. I've come to not even respect my husband because he can't seem to see how he doesn't support me and is actually doing harm to our daughter by giving her everything she needs to stay home. Not holding her accountable. Everything is a fight."

When alienation and emotional disconnection from a spouse are experienced, the relationship will weaken from resentment and loneliness. Even if we have supportive friendships, we expect and desire to feel that connection in our primary relationships as well. A stressful parental role with a non-thriving child can unearth previously unattended to dynamics within the marriage or partnership. If a couple does not know how to support each other, stay united as a couple, deal with conflict between themselves, or reach out for the other to help sooth their own pain, the stress of difficult parenting situations will expose the relationship to threat.

Stan Tatkin discusses "thirds" in a committed relationship dynamic. (Solomon & Tatkin, 2011a) Many circumstances can create a third: a mother-in-law, a pet, friends, and certainly a difficult situation with a child. Taking care of each other is the primary job of each partner especially during stress. This can easily seem contradictory to the idea that the child should come first. However, without a strong sense of partnership, energy for a non-thriving child lessens and the primary relationship is diminished. The situation with the child becomes the stressor that activates a deficit in the couple's ability to stay attuned to each other's needs and provide support while resolving conflicts.

In the most terrible of situations, when a child dies, a couple is quite vulnerable to separation because they cannot bear to experience the other's grief while enduring their own profound loss. The grief they see in the face of their partner is their own worst nightmare. What could be a more difficult time to learn how to attend to their partner's pain? The emotional connection with a partner can, however, be the strength-giving antidote to isolation, alienation, and loneliness.

Even cellular aging has been connected to social support. Dr. Elizabeth Blackburn, while working as a postdoctoral fellow at Yale University in 1975, studied the unusual nature of telomeres. Telomeres are regions at the end of each chromosome which protect the chromosome from deterioration or from fusion with neighboring chromosomes. As human telomeres shorten, cell proliferation halts, and scientists believe this process is responsible for aging at the cellular level. The most helpful visualization for me is the comparison of a telomere to the cap at the end of a shoe string. As the cap protects the shoe string from fraying, so does the telomere protect the chromosome from deterioration.

Fraying of telomeres is connected to chronic stress. Roughly one year of caring for a chronically ill child costs an individual 6 years of cellular aging. (Bredar, 2008b) Dr. Blackburn helped identify an enzyme called telomerase that repairs telomeres. Telomerase is a protein compound and an RNA primer that acts to protect the terminal ends of chromosomes.

Psychologist Elissa Epel of the University of California, San Francisco, a colleague of Dr. Blackburn, studied the telomere length of mothers of special needs children. She was interested in the effect of tending to a child with a disability on the length of telomeres and therefore escalation of the cellular aging process. The mothers studied by Epel had been meeting together with other mothers who all shared the common experience of raising a child with a disability. They had frequent meetings with each other and shared the heartbreak, the small victories, the love they felt for their children, and the shared experiences.

In Epel's study, the social affiliation and shared experience of the women with disabled children stimulated the healing effects of telomerase. The telomeres of these women were not shortened as would have been predicted given the chronically stressed situations in which they all lived. Social affiliation with those who understand, those of like mind, is a powerful tool for stress reduction and perhaps for slowing of the aging process. What a great reason to make a new friend.

Acceptance and Self-Care

All of the considerations discussed above are factors in dealing with the heartbreak of non-thriving children. It is not the children that are the heartbreak but the situations they create in our lives. They break our hearts because we love them, because we have such a strong empathic connection to them, and because their situations or behaviors are often not within our control and sometimes not within our understanding.

Acceptance of the reality that sometimes, despite our best efforts and our most heartfelt wish for the well-being of our children, there are real limits to what we can do to help. In certain situations, acceptance of limits may actually trigger increased responsibility, growth and well-being on the part of both the child and the parent. For parents to believe they have unlimited reach is a fantasy that can lead to anger, resentment and discouragement.

The ability to focus on both physical and emotional self-care can free parents to create a small space between themselves and their children. This distance can create a degree of perspective and the possibility of creating new pathways to solutions. A modicum of distance might reduce the number of sleepless nights. Differentiation is a concept I will discuss many times throughout this book. It involves creating a breathing space for a parent regardless of the intensity of the stressors. In this breathing space, a parent may be able to embrace behavioral strategies to turn off or reduce the stress response for at least intervals of time; time much needed to repair the damaging effects of prolonged stress.

These behavioral strategies include care for the body and the mind. Creating that valuable modicum of distance, and the perspective it may offer, gives psychological space for self-care behaviors such as exercising, meditating, socializing, enjoying. These behavioral choices benefit both the body and the mind with higher self-esteem, a sense of personal control, release of endorphins which work to reduce stress and pain, and increased health benefits that derive from the positive effects on cardiovascular functioning.

Parenting a non-thriving child can shut down a healthy flow of life energy, consuming the parent with fear and pre-occupation with the stressful situation. There must be room for the parents, room for life that is connected to, but separate from, the child. Parents who can make that leap may be better equipped to promote healthy strategies for themselves and their children. In some situations, this leap is more difficult to make than in others. There is not a cookie cutter answer to something as all-encompassing as concern for the well-being of our children.

In a recent conversation with a good friend, the topic of Pilates came up. She said that she had for a long time been thinking about starting to attend a Pilates class but just had not done it. I mentioned to her that activities such as yoga and Pilates help decrease inflammation and that inflammation has been linked to many disease processes such as cancer. (I'm a lot of fun to be around.) She said, "Oh, then I'm going to do it." The difference in her motivation had to do with the awareness that Pilates could help prevent perhaps devastating disease processes through the reduction of inflammation. She had previously thought of this as just something that would help her be in better shape.

The purpose of describing the effects of prolonged stress on our psychological and physiological well- being is to create an awareness that will hopefully motivate parents, struggling with on-going stresses, to attend to themselves as well as their children. The following chapters address the need to attend to prolonged stress as if it were a matter of life and death. Certainly the quality of life and the risk of disease and illness are at stake.

CHAPTER 2

The Stress Response

IT IS MOST likely clear by now that stress is a natural part of life. We all have it; we all deal with it in different ways. Learning to manage stress can make us stronger and hardier for the next stress that comes along. This is much like the process of building a muscle by lifting weights, making the muscle stronger by hard use and subsequent repair. The stress response is adaptive and even amazing in its fine-tuned preparation for danger.

Some stress has the positive effect of strengthening our ability to deal with further encounters with stressful situations. However when stress continues, providing no time for recovery, this fine-tuned mechanism can contribute to diseases that potentially lead to despair and even death. The potential damage to our bodies and brains when stress cannot be turned off, when there is not time for repair, is abundantly documented in medical and neuroscience literature.

The HPA Loop

Bear with me while I struggle through some neuroscience that is important to our understanding of the damaging effects of prolonged stress in the body. There are hundreds of trillion of connections in the brain, often noted as 'more than the number of stars in our galaxy.' One set of connections important in our understanding of stress is called the HPA (hypothalamus pituitary adrenal) loop or axis. This all-important stress loop is ignited when the amygdala (a set of neurons which is part of the limbic system and located deep in the brain) sounds the alarm that something intense is happening, and the hardworking stress hormones flood into the bloodstream. The alarm can go off, not just in response to fear or threat of some kind, but also in response to winning the lottery. The amygdala's job is to appraise the intensity of the incoming information and then send off messages that tell the adrenal gland to release hormones.

Even a subconscious perception or memory can trigger a stress response, because the input from the amygdala can bypass the thinking part of the brain (the prefrontal cortex). Within ten milliseconds of the alarm going off, the amygdala fires messages which tell the adrenal gland to release stress hormones at different stages.

First, the adrenal gland is activated to release the hormone adrenalin into the bloodstream. So our breathing, heart rate, and blood pressure increase and we experience an uncomfortable, agitated effect. Even the blood vessels of the skin are constricted to prevent too much bleeding. The next time you are under significant stress, you might notice the hair on your arms standing up straight. Finally, adrenalin prompts the release of glucose which results in the release of fatty acids which provides an increase in energy.

At the same time all of this is happening, signals are traveling from the amygdala to the hypothalamus to the pituitary gland, which activates another part of the adrenal gland, which releases the other powerful stress hormone, cortisol. This messenger pathway from the hypothalamus to the pituitary gland to the adrenal gland is called the HPA axis. This axis is key to both releasing and turning off the stress response. That is why it is so important in our understanding of how we can affect the turn-off valve and avoid living with prolonged stress hormones in our bloodstream.

The HPA is a feedback loop. The hypothalamus sends a hormone (CRH) to the pituitary gland, which sends a hormone (ACTH) to the adrenal gland, which activates the hormone adrenalin into the bloodstream. The HPA is a complex set of feedback interactions that is a major part of the neuroendocrine system that controls our reactions to stress.

One of the effects of prolonged stress is that an abundance of energy goes to supporting our system to be on alert. Therefore certain functions such as digestion, reproduction, growth and the immune system, that are not vital to deal with the immediate stress alarm, go dormant. Think of the alarm going off at a fire station. Everyone wakes up, slides down the pole, jumps into their fireproof uniforms, adrenalin and cortisol flowing. Their blood pressure is up, their heart rate is increased, and more oxygen is sent to their muscles. They are ready to go, ready to save lives, to put out the fire.

None of the firemen are thinking cheerios and orange juice because their digestive systems go dormant so more energy can be expended where needed. Adrenalin begins converting glycogen and fatty acids into glucose to fuel the muscles and brain. Endorphins are released to blunt pain. The bronchial tubes of the lungs dilate to carry more oxygen to the muscles. Blood vessels in the skin constrict to minimize bleeding. The body is totally alert and ready for action. When the fire is out, the stress hormones are no longer needed and the body can relax. Now it's time for cheerios and orange juice.

With psychological stress, there is often no pole to slide down, no truck to get into, no fire to put out. There is no outlet for all that energy buildup and release of stored fat. While under prolonged emotional stress when we cannot turn off the alarm, we do not think as clearly and our ability to regulate mood is compromised. The hippocampus, the part of the brain most responsible for memory, is affected while under prolonged stress. Bruce McEwen states, "Because the hippocampus has many receptors for cortisol to make sure we can remember what is threatening, it leaves the hippocampus vulnerable to high or chronically elevated levels of cortisol, and therefore memory and thinking processes can be negatively affected..." (McEwen, 2002) Clear thinking and memory are enhanced with the alert state that is associated with short-term stress, but chronic or long-term stress interferes with and impairs both of those functions.

We also suffer from prolonged actions of cortisol on metabolism. Cortisol converts protein into glycogen and begins to store fat. This process leads to the accumulation of fat around the abdomen. These stores of energy which are triggered by prolonged stress never get used and the body does not have a chance to recover. Fat around the abdomen puts us at greater health risks than do deposits of fat in other parts of the body. And let's face it, these fat deposits don't look good and can be a source of frustration in our attempt to deal with it.

The amygdala plays an important role in emotions and the appraisal of emotions. As prolonged stress continues, the amygdala just keeps firing. This appraisal role of the amygdala becomes increasingly sensitized and begins to feed on itself as more and more of life situations are evaluated as stressful. This engages the amygdala to call for more stress hormones and the feedback loop continues with no opportunity to recover. John J. Ratey, clinical associate professor at Harvard Medical School, writes about the cascading of stress on the brain. "Positive and realistic thoughts become less accessible, and eventually brain chemistry can shift toward anxiety or depression." (Ratey, 2008a)

To repeat, the body and brain are set up to accommodate short-term stress, not long-term stress. During an emergency, many physiological changes take place. The body is quite efficient in mobilizing energy during a crisis. These physiological changes, in fact, enable an average individual to lift a car to free a child, or to run after a burglar, not noticing that they have themselves been wounded. These are short-term stress responses that allow the body to provide us with extraordinary capacity to respond to crisis. However, if we do not put the car down soon or tend to our wound in a timely manner, harm will come to us.

Obviously, this short-term stress response is critical to our survival. Addison's disease is an example of what happens when the stress response cannot be turned on. During a crisis, someone with untreated Addison's disease will experience lowered blood pressure to the point of going into shock. We need the stress response to deal with physical and emotional crisis. We need the stress response to just get up in the morning.

Sapolsky discusses the many deleterious effects of long-term stress response on the human body. "If you experience every day as an emergency, you will pay the price." (Sapolsky, 1994c) If we do not know how to turn off the stress response, it can become more damaging than the stressor itself. Elissa Epel cites a study that measured the HPA loop in mothers who had raised children (now adults) with special needs. She found the HPA loop was no longer overactive but was instead flat and unresponsive. Cortisol was low and these mothers were suffering from burnout and exhaustion. (Epel, 2012).

The Response to Long-Term Stress

The body is incredibly efficient in the way it can speed up its heart rate, raise its blood pressure, etc. during crisis, but this is not helpful on a chronic, long-term basis. Decrease in energy, lowered immunity, susceptibility to infectious diseases, decline in sexual interest, and propensity to depression are only some of many ways people might pay a price for an activated long-term stress response. With non-thriving children, parents have no trouble activating the stress response. Turning it off becomes a more perplexing task. If the crisis does not end, how do we turn off the stress response?

Rita, a 45 year old patient, has a daughter, Jennifer, who repeatedly failed to finish a college semester because of anxiety and mental illness. Rita was struggling without a definitive diagnosis to explain her daughter's sudden non-thriving and unmotivated behavior. Jennifer spent her time in her room seemingly unmotivated to move forward. Finally, as Rita said, she "got some relief" when her daughter found a part-time, seasonal job. However, when Jennifer came home from her job, her words and mood triggered alarms for Rita. Her amygdala was always on alert. Rita appraised her daughter's account of the workday as dangerous. "My daughter said she thought she moved slower than her co-workers." Those words triggered a stress response from Rita. Her amygdala appraised this information as 'trouble to come.' Any encouraging behaviors and words were background noise because all of her antennas were alert to bad news. The HPA feedback loop continued without a chance for recovery, thereby increasing the possibility of misappraisals.

The hypothalamus is a master endocrine control center. By way of the pituitary gland, "the hypothalamus sends and receives hormones throughout the body..." (Siegel, 2010a) As mentioned earlier, when we are stressed, we secrete cortisol into our bodies, supplying energy to deal with crisis. This is an adaptive response to deal with short-term stress, but it can cause a problem when we are dealing with a chronically overwhelming situation that seems out of our control. When we live with chronic stress, the stress hormones become elevated not just to respond to a crisis but spike even in the face of minor stresses.

A couple came to therapy because they were dealing with their young son's recently diagnosed life threatening illness. Even though there was nothing particular they could do at the moment, neither of them felt they could go back to work because the on-going stress (anxiety, confusion, fear) made it impossible for them to competently attend to critically important work tasks. They were correct in that assessment (even though their employers disagreed with them) because under prolonged stress, our capacity for clear thinking, even regarding matters not associated directly with the stressor, can be diminished and our HPA loop will be easily triggered.

Allostasis And Allostatic Load

The term allostasis refers to the active process by which the body responds to daily events and maintains homeostasis or balance. The word literally means achieving stability through change. The stress response plays a necessary role in adaptation. However, here lies the inherent paradox: The systems that react to stress—the autonomic nervous system and the adrenocortical system--are important protectors of the body in the short run (fleeing from danger) but they cause damage and accelerate disease when they are active over long periods of time (prolonged sense of helplessness.) Worries about non-thriving children keep parents in stress for the long run. The price we pay physiologically and emotionally for the body's inability to turn off the stress response is called allostatic load.

As an example, we need an increase in blood pressure to get ourselves up in the morning. Blood pressure will rise and fall during the day depending on changing emotional and physical demands. This is an example of allostasis; the body adapting to change. However, continuous high blood pressure as a response to prolonged stress can promote several disease processes such as atherosclerotic plaques. The conclusion from a study published in the American Journal of Cardiology was, "Psychosocial stress contributes to high blood pressure and subsequent cardiovascular morbidity and mortality." (Schneider. et. al. 2005). This is an example of allostatic load, the inability to turn off the stress response and its accompanying physiological consequence.

Limbic Sensitivity

High levels of stress hormones in the body can not only create risk for physical disease and illness but can be toxic to the brain and interfere with neural tissue. And, more relevant to the heartbreak situations with children, chronically elevated stress hormones sensitize limbic reactivity. This means that even minor stresses become more difficult to address and emotional balance in dealing with these situations becomes more difficult to achieve. One of my patients said this well: "I am overloaded and can't take another setback." Actually, this person's limbic system is sensitized and is appraising even minor disruptions or concerns as an alarm. Dan Siegel states, "Finding a way to soothe excessively reactive limbic firing is crucial to rebalancing emotions and diminishing the harmful effects of chronic stress." (Siegel, 2010b)

So how do we soothe excessively reactive limbic firing? In other words, how do we let go of the sensitized vigilance we develop when experiencing our children as not thriving? A patient recently said to me, when explaining how she felt about her very young son's anxiety meltdowns at school and at home, "Nothing is worse than watching your child suffering." I hear it over and over again.

These parents have difficulty finding feeling words for their experience. There is nothing else that seems to compare. It is a syndrome, so to speak. It is a compilation of fear, dread, anxiety, sometimes shame and embarrassment, a sense of having no control, catastrophic expectations, powerlessness, impending doom, sometimes guilt and disappointment, loss, grief, and so many other difficult feelings. Every word I have used above is a direct quote from patients who parent heartbreak kids, regardless of the age.

31

So once again, how do we soothe excessive limbic firing? This is a difficult question to answer. And I would never want to suggest that there is one strategy, or one action to take, that will be helpful in all of the heartbreaking situations that involve the lives of our children. It is the deepest pain I have seen in my patients. However, the first step for parents is gaining a clear understanding that the prolonged stress they experience is dangerous to *their* health and needs attention. They need a perspective that empowers them, provides a differentiation between themselves and the struggles or behaviors of their children. (That does not imply a giving up or a lack of attention to their children's issues.) When at all possible, they need the ability to make space between the situation and their response, so they are not consumed by their emotions. This provides an opportunity to respond receptively rather than reactively to behaviors and situations. So, parents in heartbreaking situations need tools that allow them to react to the intensity of the situation without being consumed by it.

Self-Soothing

To create that all important space between the stressful situation and the parent's response depends on the ability to self-soothe. It's a valuable skill in all interpersonal relationships, and the stronger the emotions elicited, the more essential self-soothing becomes. A pre-requisite to differentiation, as discussed in the previous chapter, is the ability to self-soothe.

Self-soothing is a regulatory strategy that enhances the ability to attend to your own feelings without reactivity or personalization *and*, at the same time, be available to the experiences of another person. In our context, of course, that someone else is the source of much love and much anguish. Self-soothing requires awareness of how the stress mechanism is affecting your body and the development of tools to reduce its damaging effects.

There are many ways to strengthen self-soothing skills. One is breathing. It is quite useful to learn and practice how to use your breath as a source for anxiety reduction. It is a powerful tool and easy enough to master. Take a minute to try this simple and commonly used exercise: Place your hands on your diaphragm; that spot on top of the "V" where your ribs come together. Breathe in through your nose and fill up that area where your hands are, like filling a balloon, and hold your breath for a few counts. Breathe out through your mouth with a slight sound, making the exhalation slow and deliberate. Slowly deflate the balloon of air. A common practice is to inhale slowly for 6 counts, hold for two counts and exhale for 8 counts. The exhale is slightly longer than the inhale because it is the exhale that informs your brain that everything is alright; no need to send down the stress hormones. Your inhale brings energy; your exhale brings calmness by reducing your heart rate and increasing oxygen to the brain. In that state, it is easier to regulate emotions, which enhances a receptive rather than a reactive response to stressful situations. Self-soothing skills empower an individual to make room to reflect, to gain perspective and clarity in responsiveness. That is the receptive state of mind which is so valuable when facing long-term stressful situations involving the well-being of our children.

Other strategies for self-soothing and achieving greater regulation of emotional states are presented in the following chapters. The emotional and physiological effects of prolonged stress can be altered and approaches that help us achieve an empowering perspective and develop strategies for our own self-care can be learned.

As anyone reading this book knows, there are no easy or simple answers that apply to all situations. Dealing with a chronically or terminally ill child will most likely elicit quite different emotions than dealing with a child who is oppositional and abusive. Dealing with a child who is mentally ill might have quite different emotional aspects than dealing with a child with a developmental disorder. However, what these situations have in common is the heartbreak for parents. There is not one answer. There are, however, strategies that can empower parents with new perspectives and perhaps new tools that can significantly address the effects of prolonged stress on their bodies and their lives. All of which, actually, can help parents be increasingly effective and available to their children. Although this is a paradigm-like shift in perspective for parents, it can be accomplished. As parents become more knowledgeable about the effects of stress on their body/brain, and as they acquire protective tools, they become more effective and emotionally regulated.

CHAPTER 3

The Empathic Connection

"I CRASH WHEN she crashes," was a statement of helplessness made by my patient Rita who had recently brought her daughter back from yet another failed attempt to make it through a full semester of college. Her daughter, Jennifer, experienced "breakdowns" that were ultimately diagnosed as bipolar disorder. Jennifer was prescribed medications that now seemed encouraging. She and her family held hope that by fall semester she would be stable enough to return and succeed at college.

However, fall quarter was too soon for Jennifer, and the positive effects of the medications that had held such promise were diminishing. Jennifer spent most of her time in her room, showing no motivation for movement of any kind. She began a part time job which lasted only a few months. All hopes now turned to winter quarter. Although Rita had a support system, did regular physical exercise, and worked a busy schedule, her emotional life always teetered on her daughter's daily emotional and behavioral state.

"I crash when she crashes" described the predominate and pervasive emotional force in her life. This emotional state dampened joys and escalated fears and concerns. Will Jennifer be ready for school next quarter? Will I get the dreaded call from school saying she needs to come home? If so, what will she do? How will I cope with her sleeping all morning with no motivation or goals? What do I do with all this anxiety that I wake up to each morning?

The empathic connection to our children has us basking in their joys and successes. Even their smallest accomplishments fill us with pride. That is why we carry their pictures in our wallets (I mean on our smart phones.) They are a part of us. We can weather their failures and missteps easily enough as long as their futures are not at stake. We need to envision their prosperity and well-being in order to relax into parenting and into our own lives.

All caring parents struggle with holding on and letting go of control. Is she old enough to spend the night with a friend? Should she be dating yet? Is he responsible enough to drive that long trip by himself? Can I still have a say in the friends he has chosen? Ideally, we make these decisions based on the maturity of our children. As we watch them grow and become competent young people, we gradually let go. We cannot help but notice that we soon will not have any control and we better just get used to it. And we love it. We want to move into different stages of parenting, even though each changing stage is accompanied with loss. We want our children to take over their lives. We want them to be in control of their destiny. We want them to thrive.

And what if they are not thriving? What if they don't leave home? What if their behaviors are manipulative, hurtful or abusive? What if, for whatever reasons, they don't take care of themselves? What if they withdraw from life, having few friends or resources? What if they embark on lives that put themselves or others in danger? What if they suffer from mental illness and will not comply with treatment? What if they demonstrate no motivation to be independent? What if they are cut off from a social network and have only you? What if they have nowhere to go but home?

There are, of course, far more situations than listed above that provide the material for a parent's nightmare: a child not thriving, not able or willing to take control of his life, or whose behavior is hurtful. Can a parent with a strong empathic connection ("I crash when she crashes") move through the nightmare into acceptance and self-care? That is not what a parent with a distressed child typically asks about when they come to therapy. They ask about what they can do for their son or daughter. And of course they would. They would do anything to help their child thrive as any good parent would do. There is often too much pain, anxiety and fear to consider the idea of acceptance and self-care.

Dr. Mairi Harper from Science and Technology Policy Research found that bereaved mothers in Wales and England were up to four times more likely to die in the decade after their child's death. A very sad statistic. How does grief kill? There is reason to believe that the stress of bereavement may suppress the immune system and therefore increase a person's propensity to disease. Although many factors come into play with the loss of a child, Dr. Harper implicates the impact of stress. She states, "My own personal opinion is that parents don't get anywhere near the level of support and understanding they need to cope." (Harper, 2011)

Furthermore, the empathic connection to a loved one's pain or "merely knowing your loved one is suffering," as stated by a team of researchers from University College London, is enough to activate pain centers in the brain. Dr. Tani Singer, lead researcher of the study in London, states "We use emotional representations reflecting our own subjective feeling states to understand the feelings of others" and particularly those we love. (Singer, 2014) In other words, my fear about my son's loneliness triggers my own ideas and feelings about being alone in the world and may activate implicitly held memories of my own early experiences. It becomes difficult to differentiate between my own held memories and projections and my child's experiences.

Empathy has at least two essential ingredients. First is the capacity to understand and relate to the other person's emotional state. And second is the cognitive capacity to experience the other person's state while differentiating between self and other. So there lies the problem for parents. How do you keep self and other (my child) differentiated? "I crash when she crashes" informs us of the extreme difficulty keeping any degree of separation between our children's struggles or behaviors and our own emotional reactions. Differentiation becomes a needed skill, which I will address in more detail in later chapters.

A friend of mine came to work many years ago noticeably distressed. It was his 5 year old daughter's first day of kindergarten. She didn't want to go. She was afraid and would have preferred to stay home. He left her in tears. My friend carried his daughter's distress and tears all day. He rushed home to meet her after school, anticipating the need to comfort her and rally her on to give the next day a try, only to find a very happy little girl who had been delighted at her first day experience.

Her emotions that morning and the prior evening had manifested in him what first day of kindergarten often manifests in parents: the difficulty letting go of control and protection. He could not be there to help her, to wipe away the tears. For this day, he could not make it alright for her. His pain that day was not her pain. His pain was the reality that he couldn't help her and protect her always. Her pain was just first day of school jitters.

"I crash when she crashes," is a parent's helplessness speaking. "I can't fix it. I don't know what else to do." Our empathic connection to our children's pain is seasoned with our own negative forecast of their future and our inability to fix it. When deeply enmeshed in their children's struggles, parents work so hard for solutions, only to find themselves with little if any control over the suffering or problematic behavior. They also experience the deeply felt loss of control of their own emotional well-being.

"I crash when she crashes" is what we have all experience as loving, empathic parents. However, when the crashes take over the emotional life of a parent, the ability to stay centered and emotionally regulated is weakened and, in this state, the parent becomes less of a resource for the child. Parents in these situations lose the ability to differentiate their own emotional state from their child's.

We are "wired to connect" to others. Reactivity to the pain of others is associated with a region of the brain called the anterior cingulate cortex. Of course, that part of the brain is more activated when we observe a member of our own family or social group in pain. We are wired that way. When the pain we see lies within our children, it becomes more complicated. It is essential to a parent's peace of mind to be able to forecast a positive future for their children. Our empathy overloads us with fear and dread when we forecast our child not thriving. The empathic connection is there. It is strong. It can be all encompassing. On one hand, it is the basis of healthy relationships. And on the other hand, empathy without differentiation can weaken our own boundaries and sense of direction.

We are not looking to reduce our empathic connection to our children. We are looking to strengthen the ability to differentiate, so that we as parents can draw upon resources of clarity, stability, flexibility, problem solving, and self-care, thereby increasing our ability to be worthy resources for our children. If we crash when they crash, we reduce our ability to respond. When we reduce our ability to respond with clarity and flexibility, we increase our risk of helplessness and depression. Depression and helplessness often exist side by side. Both states are disempowering and lessen our ability to stay present with current situations and make clearly thought out responses.

Barbara, whose 24 year old daughter was unmotivated and emotionally damaged from earlier childhood experiences with her estranged father, came into her session joyfully discussing how she had begun hanging pictures on the mostly empty walls of a house that she and her family had moved into 5 years ago. She had purchased new towels for the guest bathroom as well as a new comforter for the extra bedroom. Why now? Her daughter had applied for and was chosen for a seasonal job in a fabric store.

Barbara told me how she could not justify having such a nice house and spending time and money on making it complete while her daughter struggled with lack of movement in her life, loneliness and social isolation. Now there was hope, and therefore, she could hang pictures. She was so entangled in her daughter's suffering that she and the rest of the family were caught under the heavy cloud of restricted happiness.

Our empathic connection and emotional attunement to our children are essential for healthy attachment to take place. A secure attachment is at the core of a child's emotional and interpersonal well-being. Building a secure base for a child depends on the parent's ability to attune to the child's emotional state. "Empathy is the real-time experiencing of another's sorrow, anguish, or pain as if it were happening to oneself." (Solomon & Tatkin, 2011b) So the empathic connection provides the basis for attunement and the prospect of secure attachment to our children which is essential to their well-being.

It is that same experience of empathic connection that becomes so difficult when our children do not achieve developmental, interpersonal, physical, or psychological health or behave in ways that break our hearts. How do we regulate our own emotional pain and attune to our own needs when the pull of our children's distress is so magnetic?

Navigating through encompassing emotions such as dread, fear, panic, anxiety, anger, and frustration requires that we hold the belief that two things are possible: First, that we can expand our capacity to tolerate these difficult emotions, and second, that we can, at the same time, maintain or build a capacity for vitality, energy, aliveness, and flexibility in our own lives. This is what Dan Siegel refers to as "widening the window of tolerance." (Siegel, 2010c) If our children's happiness is on the line and our ability to help or influence seems limited, our "window of tolerance" can be quite narrow. This subject will be expanded upon in later chapters.

If we believe we cannot bear the pain, we will build a defense to protect us from that pain. The defense may be of the fight, flight, or freeze options. It is important to remember that all of these defenses work well in certain threatening situations. The animal posing as dead (the freeze defense) may save himself from the animal that is one up on the food chain and looking for dinner. Running or fighting (if we have the ability to do either) can certainly save a life under threat. However, as we shut down or run from (avoid) emotional pain, we also shut down our window to the alive, energizing emotions so central to well-being. If we shut down one area of emotional aliveness, we will also experience restriction in our broader emotional awareness and expressiveness.

The strong empathic connection works in both directions. "When she flies, I fly." When a non-thriving child takes seemingly the smallest step forward, a parent will not only be elated and hopeful but also able to turn down the stress response. The more parents can recognize and stay open for those small steps, the more opportunities will arise for reducing the hormonal effects of long-term stress and thereby decrease the fight-flight-freeze responses to what seems unbearable pain and worry.

Richard, the father of an adult daughter whose social anxiety prevented her from moving forward to college or a job or really anything outside her room and whose social contacts were limited to online interactions, was told by his daughter that she had met a young man online and would like to invite him over for dinner. Richard was thrilled, one could say ecstatic, with the possibility that his daughter's life might expand. And it has.

Although, "when she flies, I fly" is a source of relief and joy for a parent, emotions tied solely to the experiences of the child can exacerbate rather than reduce the stress cycle. Although it is important to take in the small (or large) victories, parents need a full cadre of positive experiences that are connected to their own life style choices not just to the positive and negative experiences of their children.

Empathy and Attunement Between Parents

Interestingly, research done by UCLA psychologist Shelley Taylor argues that the flight-fight response to stress may be more applicable to males than females. (Taylor, 2000) She contends that since females are generally less aggressive than males and often have the responsibility of caring for children, their response to stress is more "tend and befriend" than fight or flight. By "tend" she is addressing the caring and protection of children and by "befriend" she is referring to the forming of a cohesive group of women who offer support and understanding. (Geary et. al., 2000)

Taylor's work indicates that during stress, women may turn more to important relationships for comfort which is indeed a positive coping mechanism. If your best friend is your spouse, as is wonderful to experience, that best friend may also be engulfed with the same worries and concerns but handling it differently (for instance: avoidance, denial or inattentiveness).

The state of the relationship between two parents of a non-thriving child is vulnerable to non-attunement. Both partners in a couple who are attuned to each other can anticipate what will be upsetting to their partner and how best to provide comfort. They know how to enhance positive moments and minimize (not avoid) negative moments that their partner experiences.

However, the heartbreak of a child's struggle can make it difficult for each partner to listen empathically to the pain of the other. Blame, avoidance, and disagreements will distance partners from each other. A sense of abandonment and helplessness weigh heavily on a couple's ability to communicate compassion and empathy for each other—to be each other's best friend. Both desperately need each other but often respond to their situation with distancing and non-attuned behavior. The other's pain seems too much to bear, since this very pain is their own worst nightmare. I have realized in my work with these parents how difficult it is for them to attend to their own friendships, health, and even (sometimes particularly) the relationships with their spouses.

Couples need help and support to keep their relationship primary— even primary to the non-thriving child. When one or both parents are preoccupied with the child, at the cost of attunement to their spouse, the child-parent relationship can become the primary relationship, thus superseding and overshadowing the primacy of the couple relationship. In a two parent family, the security of the couple is essential to provide a secure, consistent, self-regulated base for the child.

This can be a difficult concept. The couple I discussed earlier who came to therapy to address how they together were dealing with their very young son's frightening medical diagnosis demonstrated a remarkable attunement to each other and an ability to keep the relationship primary. She had taken a leave of absence from her job, and he was working very flexible hours to be available both to his son in the hospital and to their older daughter. The couple had agreed that all their time and energy belonged to both children. They worked together; staying incredibly attuned to each other's needs and to taking care of themselves enough to manage this very traumatic experience. They supported each other's need to take time to exercise. They talked about how they each processed the stress differently and could be there for the other's "meltdown."

This was a couple who was collaborative, differentiated from one another (in that they understood and accepted that they processed their emotions differently), attuned to each other, and able to hold the other's pain, knowing that the same would be done for them. They were open vessels for suggestions and ideas. I present this couple because they are a model of keeping their relationship primary without compromising the needs of their children. Obviously, their strong attunement to each other's needs has helped each of them have the energy to be responsive to the needs of both children.

Partners who are dealing with some form of non-thriving in their children benefit from experiencing their partner as being attuned to their feelings and available to provide comfort. Communication needs to encompass the ability to take the other's view into account without defensiveness and to know how to protect their partner against mistreatment by the child or anyone else. Each partner's job is to cover the other's back—even against their own child. This is particularly difficult if the couple has not developed strong communication skills earlier in their relationship. The behaviors of their child might be the opportune trigger to seek couples' therapy.

The ability to respond less out of threat or fear or helplessness widens our window of tolerance, thus widening our capacity to stay attentive to our own emotional world—both painful and joyful. Attaching solely to the stress of heartbreak parenting reduces not only our aliveness and vitality but also our effective availability to our children. Try as we must, there are pains we cannot eliminate or reduce. We can, however, embrace the notion that it is possible to build the capacity to bear difficult emotions by attending to our own emotional and physical needs. By doing so we become more available to see clearly and to respond effectively to those we love.

CHAPTER 4

Turning Off the Stress Response

Acceptance

WE WILL NOT, and cannot, accept the idea that our children may not experience the happiness we so much want for them. Rita's daughter returned once again to try another college semester. She had failed several times to complete a semester, returning home with signs of mental illness. When Rita was informed by the college that Jennifer had again experienced an emotional breakdown and would not be able to finish fall semester, Rita immediately resumed her search for an answer and a treatment. That search culminated in a different diagnosis than Jennifer had received after the previous meltdown during spring semester.

This diagnosis was even more troubling than the first diagnosis. However, medication was changed and prospects for stability were improved. As those prospects rather rapidly dwindled, however, the search for an answer resumed. Rita needed a diagnosis that would give her hope that her daughter would live a normal life, a life that would be at least sprinkled with a flavor of happiness.

Rita's life had all the ingredients to be fulfilled and happy. She was close to an early retirement, had a good relationship with her husband, was a well-respected professional in the community, had interests and ambitions, and had ample finances to support her lifestyle. And yet, she woke every morning and went to bed every night with what she called "a gripping sense of terror" about what would happen in her daughter's life and, therefore, to her life. As she came to accept Jennifer's diagnosis, she began asking different questions. How will *I* be able to live my life? Am I supposed to accept this diagnosis? How do I do that? How can I have happiness if she can't?

How can I have happiness if she can't? We want our children to be better educated than we are, more prosperous than we are, taller and better looking than we are, at least as happy if not happier in their relationships than we are. We just want them to be thriving in whatever way makes them happy.

The situations that I have been addressing that preempt our children from being happy in the ways we have envisioned for them, force us to look differently at their lives and our connection to their lives. In fact, the difference is a paradigm-like shift. This shift in perspective involves deciding what to accept and what to keep fighting for.

Rita desperately wanted Jennifer to "be the way she used to be." Jennifer's behavior (spending most of her time sequestered in her room, overeating, and displaying a lack of motivation) was extremely frustrating to Rita. Rita spent much of her emotional energy trying to change those frustrating behaviors. Her question to herself was, "Why does she do this to herself?" She would start many sentences with, "If she would just…."

In spite of evidence to the contrary, Rita kept her hope that Jennifer would return to school and persevere through graduation. Jennifer did return to school for winter semester and dropped out in early March. The phone call from the counseling center at her college was devastating to both of her parents. A new way to view their daughter's well-being had to begin. It would not be acceptable to Rita and her husband to allow Jennifer to stay home, spending most of her time in her room on the computer. However, college was no longer an option, and her prospects for a job seemed slim. "What am I supposed to do?" was Rita's question to me.

The answer to this haunting parental question lies in the premise that there are circumstances in our children's lives that we as parents cannot set right. We will try. We will do our best. We would sacrifice mightily if it would alter painful circumstances. Over and over I see parents who have come to realize that their attempt at direct intervention in the lives of their non-thriving children does not produce a different outcome. In fact, in some circumstances, that attempt can increase the strain on the relationship.

Acceptance is a tough concept for a parent to grasp while watching their child struggle with life. Behaviors that are self-destructive, such as Jennifer's overeating with a diabetic condition, makes acceptance seem not only inappropriate but impossible. The emotional and cognitive process of acceptance is far different than its dictionary definition. Acceptance, in this circumstance, does not mean acquiescence, or concurrence, or approval, or agreement. It *does* mean knowing what you can and cannot make right or fix or control. It means looking at things as they are instead of how we think they should be. Acceptance requires coming into the present moment and responding to what is.

After many frustrating and anxious months, Rita worked hard to accept that her daughter now had a restricted capacity for work. She had hoped that Jennifer would find a job that would allow her to use her high intelligence but Jennifer was in no way capable of that kind of job requirement, even though she is an intellectually gifted young woman. This growing acceptance helped Rita direct her focus on seeking "anything that will give Jennifer structure and get her out of her room."

Through the assistance of a state agency, that "anything..." turned out to be a 3-day a week job doing factory work. Rita, although heartbroken at the present situation, sees this as a step. She will, of course, be looking for indications that Jennifer can move along a path to more fulfilling work. Letting go of the "If she would just....." has freed Rita, in subtle ways, from the intense frustration she was experiencing. Her acceptance has not changed the heartbreak, but her responses to her daughter are more effective.

This is obviously not the life Rita had envisioned for her exceptionally bright daughter, but the hope is that the job program might provide an attainable goal. It took Rita's acceptance that, for now, she could not help Jennifer be "like she used to be." She had to let go of certain expectations and work with her own sorrow and loss. Acceptance often involves addressing intense grief.

Rita must always have a plan B, in case this one doesn't work. Whatever the plan, it needs to accommodate the necessity for her and her husband to live without debilitating long-term stress. Jennifer's circumstance will most likely create short-term stressors for the family and will most likely be accompanied by heartbreak. Hopefully, the heartbreak will be a shorter term response made easier with acceptance and the provision of attainable goals.

Another example of acceptance in the midst of heartbreak is Laura, whose son, Josh, was diagnosed with schizophrenia when he was 19. Laura took every path available to procure help for her son Josh, but none of her actions altered the course of his mental illness or his behavior with her.

When I first saw Laura in my practice, Josh was 31, actively drinking and non-compliant with medication. She dreaded each phone call from her son and particularly hoped these disturbing calls would not come at night. She began not answering his calls for fear he would be drinking and begging to come to her house. This made her feel guilty and sad for the rest of the night. She would not talk about him to friends for fear of their judgment of her. She did not know if her son was living on the streets or in a church basement. Incarceration for violent behavior had not resulted in a change in his non-compliance. Laura's worry increased as she had less and less contact with Josh. She felt lonely herself and resented that she could not have a relationship with her son.

The paradigm change, for Laura, came as she began to assess that there was nothing she could do to positively change his situation. If a new opportunity arose, she would jump to take advantage of it. However, short of Josh being willing to cooperate with treatment, there was nothing she could do. In her acceptance of that reality, Laura has been able to clearly express her boundaries to Josh, finding ways to offer help without putting herself in jeopardy. This position has provided her with enough of a sense of safety that she can now talk to him without the same level of anxiety and fear.

Laura will meet Josh at a public location and buy him lunch. She will leave if he becomes loud or threatening to her or anyone in the restaurant. She will always offer to take him to a program or a hospital and will provide him with gift certificates to his favorite fast food restaurants, but she will not provide cash. Laura is sad and upset every time she has contact with Josh. That will never change as long as his situation remains the same. However, she moves on faster and with less guilt or long-term stress each time she sees him or talks to him by phone or email. (She has provided him with a cell phone to help her feel less anxious regarding his whereabouts.)

This is an important point about acceptance. As Laura began to accept her limitation in helping her son get better treatment and be safer out there in the world, her responses changed. She was able to get relief from the HPA loop long enough to pause and respond receptively rather than reactively. She gained that all-important pause that helped her react with less self-blame and fewer catastrophic thoughts. She developed more acceptance of what she can and cannot do. The interesting paradox is, of course, that by achieving a somewhat subtle change in her thinking and behaving she has become more accessible and effective in dealing with her son. Therefore, an upward spiral was created.

The only behavior she could change was her own. No matter how many times she let him spend the night with his promise of no alcohol, he could not comply. No matter how many times she gave him money for food (not drugs) or took him to a program, he could not comply. Her acceptance involved the reality that she could not impact his choices; however, she could create boundaries to reduce her fear. She did not answer calls beyond a certain time of night, since his calls were often upsetting and no action on her part could help him. She would not have a conversation if he had been drinking.

Her accessibility to him increased as she confidently adhered to her boundaries. His desire to communicate with her appeared to increase, and she now was able to express her caring for him. If he wants a small job at her house he must be sober. If he acts out in a restaurant, she will leave. Laura knows what she can and cannot do and works toward reducing long-term sadness, guilt, and heartbreak after each visit with him. She has empowered herself to be more available to him because she trusts her boundaries. This increase in connection with him reduces guilt for her. The less guilt and sadness each visit provokes, the more comfortable she can be with direct contact with Josh. All the better for Josh to have his mother's increased availability to him.

Differentiation

Another aspect of the paradigm change involves the concept of differentiation that I discussed in the Heartbreak chapter. Beth, a 37-year-old patient, is a good example of the usefulness of differentiation. Years ago, Beth had taken on the responsibility for her older schizophrenic sister with no support from other family members. This responsibility had become a predominant expenditure of her time and energy. She had not married up to that point, but had recently become engaged to a 40-year-old man. She was now having difficulty integrating her responsibilities for her sister into her upcoming marriage.

To have a successful relationship with her husband-to-be, she would need to integrate him into her own life rather than define her life by her sister's needs. Beth's life had become deeply entrenched in the pursuit of her sister's happiness, or at least, her sister's comfort. To have a healthy relationship in her upcoming marriage, learning to differentiate *her* life from the responsibility of tending to her sister, and acknowledging her own need to "make up for the other family members' neglect," became an important step in reclaiming a life for herself.

Beth needed a boundary with her sister, a space in-between the two of them, so she could have an intimate, committed relationship in her life AND be there for her sister in a more defined way. The goal of differentiation is not to give up the responsibilities she had taken on, but to integrate those responsibilities into her own fuller life.

How do people learn to differentiate? The opposite of differentiation (in my experience) is enmeshment or entanglement, a state from which it is difficult to achieve a sense of separation. There are times (many of them) that we just cannot achieve differentiation from our children. My youngest daughter started a new and stressful job. Her first few days filled her with catastrophic thinking like, "I can't do this. There is too much to learn. I'll never find what I really want to do." So, each day I waited for a text telling me how the day went. I was so invested in this job working for her, to build her confidence, to make her happy, that I did a poor job of focusing on my own job. My questions to her each day came from my anxiety and did her no good at all. (In fact, I made her more nervous about the job.) This kind of temporary entanglement can be seen as a natural part of parenting as long as it is not the main event governing the relationship.

We can be very close, very interdependent, and very emotionally intimate in a relationship and still be differentiated. We learn to differentiate by addressing our own needs well enough to be present and attuned to the state of the other person. Beth needed to understand the adverse effect of her entanglement with her sister and move toward behaviors that reinforced the healthy position of differentiation. As she gained this insight, she began collaborating with her fiancé to set time limits on week-end visits with her sister. She began to assert herself with other family members to get help for her sister. Her fiancé, in turn, clearly understood that Beth's sister would always be a major part of her life, and therefore a reality in his life. She moved from "I am a package with my sister" to a collaborative effort to integrate her responsibility to her sister with her life with her fiancé. That collaborative problem solving was a great start to their marriage and a needed reinforcement to Beth.

Accomplishing this did not make her schizophrenic sister's life worse. That differentiation ("I have chosen to be responsible for my sister AND that is only a part of my life") created meaningful distractions from the stress of dealing with her sister's situation and made a much fuller life and source of energy for herself, her fiancé and her sister. This shift required a different way of thinking, a paradigm-like change in perspective.

Of all the significant relationships in one's life, those with children most challenge our ability to create and sustain healthy boundaries for our own lives. Maintaining healthy boundaries is difficult enough with thriving children. When we carry fear and anxiety about a child's future and well-being, or experience hurtful interactions with children, the task of attending to our own lives is encumbered with emotional obstacles.

Even though feelings of fear and anxiety, as well as the experience of being overwhelmed, will not dissipate as long as our children are struggling, the ability to differentiate ourselves from them becomes a crucial tool to keep the HPA loop from spinning. Empathy will keep us connected. Differentiation will keep us from getting stuck.

Moving along, moving forward. Just moving is the goal. Getting stuck in despair or hopelessness is the obstacle. The ability to differentiate simply helps us avoid the trap of personalization (I am failing as a parent) and co-dependency ("when she crashes, I crash") while creating space for healthy distracters. To remain a strong emotional support for non-thriving children, life has to become more than just the stressors.

Staving off the Depression Loop

Getting stuck in the stressors is psychologically dangerous. There is increasing evidence that those who get depressed as a reaction to the stressors in their lives have a difficult time recovering from those stressors. (Sapolsky, 1994d) Do you see the loop? The HPA (the neuro-chemical loop in the brain responding to stress) is activated by the negative appraisal of situations (remember, when chronically stressed, even minor stresses can activate the HPA loop.) As we assess more and more situations as stressful, we become more vulnerable to depression. The more depressed we become the more we ignite the HPA loop. In other words, the more we view events and situations from a depressed outlook, the more our bodies will respond by flooding the system with stress hormones. This promotes even more despair in someone already depressed or feeling hopeless.

Depression that is accompanied by grief and guilt can be incapacitating as individuals become overwhelmed with despair. The guilt spins into its own loop. A depressed person feels bad about being depressed and unable to be there for others. In a state of depression, all things seem even worse than they may really be. Psychologist Aaron Beck of the University of Pennsylvania describes depression as a thought disorder, meaning that depressed people begin to see the world through a mostly negative lens, exacerbated by their own negative thoughts. (Beck, 2009)

People suffering from depression often have elevated levels of glucocorticoids, the central hormone of the stress response, primarily because they are facing extraordinarily difficult emotions all held within themselves. "The world looks negative. I fight it by myself and, knowing that my child or my relationship with my child is in jeopardy, I become increasingly unable to respond effectively to the situation which only serves to heighten my depression and guilt."

There are important links between stress and depression. Stress brings about endocrine changes typical in depression. "Both stress and glucocorticoids can bring about neuro-chemical changes that have been implicated in depression." (Sapolsky, 1994e) We need tools to avoid that dangerous loop, especially when dealing with the heartbreaking situations that surround non-thriving children. A depressed parent will be less capable of responding effectively to the stressful situations generated by their children's struggles. And the loop goes on and on.

Parents who become highly anxious can get caught in distressful, swirling thoughts. Obviously, some sources of anxiety need action, not distraction. If you were alone and suddenly became aware of someone following you down a desolate street in a dangerous area of town, you would not focus attention on breathing to calm your emotions. Instead, you would move toward action—run, yell, do something to take control of the situation. However, the situations that create emotional stress rather than physical stress do not always have intuitive outlets. Building a repertoire of behaviors and thought processes that help turn off the stress response becomes essential when stressors in our lives are prolonged and continuous.

We need outlets for emotional stress. Ratey states that anyone "... will exhibit the ill effects of chronic stress if there is no outlet for frustration, no sense of control, no social support. Essentially, if there is no hope, our brains don't shut off the response." (Ratey, 2008b) Strategies to deal with the difficult heartbreaking situations we experience with non-thriving children, of any age, must allow space for hope, space for a sense of control, space for outlets that diminish the physiological and psychological dangers of prolonged stress responses.

Outlets

As discussed earlier, we cannot carry stress in our body long-term without paying a price both physiologically and psychologically. Stress can come from many sources when our children are not thriving. When the source of stress cannot be successfully addressed with an action, it becomes difficult to find an outlet to mitigate intense feelings. However, an outlet must be found if we are to maintain health and well-being and remain effectively responsive to our children's situations.

An outlet for frustration or anxiety must be something positive for you. It must have the characteristic of reminding you that there is more to life than the source of the stress. An example of an effective outlet is aerobic exercise. Exercise qualifies as an outlet because, not only does it work physiologically to counter stress, it also serves the double function of providing an aspect of life that can be under your control. Taking control is in itself a psychological outlet.

Going back to our discussion about allostasis and allostatic load (see The Stress Response chapter), the stress response prepares the body for an immediate burst of energy to respond in some physical way to a stressor. Psychological stress creates the same hormonal reactions in the body but without a physical cause. Nowhere to run, nothing to fight. Aerobic exercise provides an outlet for the increase in stress hormones that flood the body when we experience or perceive something as stressful. As the body prepares for an energy requirement, aerobic exercise gives the outlet.

Although it is important that an outlet be something that is meaningful and pleasurable to you (which is NOT how most of us view exercise), eventually its benefits will convert many disbelievers. Aerobic exercise is an outlet that helps reduce the danger that stress will lead to depression and the debilitating physiological and psychological loop that can occur. I will further discuss the protective factors provided by physical outlets in the Run For Your Life chapter.

The following chapters are essentially about finding and building outlets for stress. The prerequisite for finding outlets is the strong belief that they are indeed essential to combat the deleterious effects of prolonged stress. Outlets are about distractions, physical release of energy build-up, support from others, taking control of important areas of life, and utilizing tools to help create an emotional center. Everyone needs these outlets, but when our stress hormones are activated chronically by our frustration, fear, hurt and worry about our children, the stress will be prolonged and the need for strategies and perspective will be imperative.

In later chapters I will be talking about strategies that can help parents turn off the stress response long enough to recover physiologically; long enough to pause before reacting or interpreting an interaction or an event. These strategies include:

- gaining some degree of control over areas of life that matter.
- providing outlets for physiological buildup of long term stress.
- developing the emotional ability to respond receptively rather than reactively.
- pausing and choosing intentionally where to focus attention.
- eliciting support and recognizing the power of social affiliation when struggling with heartbreak.

"When she crashes, I crash" needs to change to "When she crashes, I know what I can and cannot do to help and then I keep moving my life along so I can be a strong support."

CHAPTER 5

Calming the Storm

LIVING IN A family with a non-thriving child directs an enormous proportion of attention to the stressors. Whether the source of the problem is addiction, mental illness, oppositional-defiant behavior, neurological or medical issues, or any situation that is restricting the child and the relationship between parent and child, life wraps around the problems and affects all surrounding relationships.

Although the brain thrives on positive experiences, negative experiences are equally powerful, in that they induce a sense of helplessness. Todd came to therapy because of depression, inattention to his work, and troubled relationships with his son, Jeffrey, and his wife. He and his wife disagreed about how to parent their oppositional adult son. Todd began to drink more than he thought he should and could not concentrate at work. Jeffrey was verbally abusive to him, which hurt him deeply. His wife was of the opinion that this was mostly Todd's fault, which added to his misery and guilt. Couple's therapy and even an attempt at family therapy did not change the family dynamic. Todd desperately needed a perspective that allowed him flexibility in how he directed his attention and a distraction from the repeated flood of negative experiences.

Todd needed to find a way to create resilience in his life by increasing his tolerance for high arousal, which he experienced most evenings at home. High arousal can be fun if you are on a roller coaster or enjoying a scary movie. Those short lived experiences of adrenalin rush can be positively stimulating. Soon you want to get off the ride and leave the movie (unless you're 15). Todd couldn't get off the ride. He understandably could not retain a stable, energized place while experiencing the repeated emotional distress of his family situation. Todd needed to live within tolerable levels of emotional arousal which would allow him to avoid self-destructive behaviors and attitudes. Todd needed to be able to respond to his son and wife with less fear, guilt or helplessness. His fear was for his son's future. His guilt was about his angry responses to his son, and his helplessness was not knowing what to do for his son, for his marriage or for himself. Todd needed to create choice for himself; choice in how he focused his attention and in how he interpreted his situation.

The excessive use of alcohol had served to not only numb the pain of Todd's family situation but had flattened his entire emotional life. We cannot deaden one part of our emotional experience without affecting the quality of aliveness in another part. His apathy at work and withdrawal from interaction with colleagues created a sense of shame and isolation.

Managing the storm of negative and frightening emotions without resorting to unhealthy life style choices, like excessive drinking, over eating, isolating and so forth, requires emotional balance. The body, mind and brain are fully equipped to assist in this pursuit of resilience, balance, and emotional regulation. You remember (of course) from the Stress Response chapter that the HPA (hypothalamic-pituitary-adrenal) axis, together with the actions from the sympathetic nervous system, sends adrenalin to the body for vitality and preparation for action.

To balance the high arousal of the sympathetic nervous system, the parasympathetic branch of the autonomic nervous system (ANS), along with the actions of the HPA, produces states of relaxation and recovery. If all goes well, we will be able to operate with alertness and calmness at the same time. This system is amazing in its capacity to keep a balance between too much and too little of both adrenaline and cortisol. This is particularly relevant to our subject in that, as Stan Tatkin states, "Optimal ANS arousal also affects the amount of available oxygen and glucose metabolism in the brain, which in turn determines our availability to process and respond to experience" (Solomon, Tatkin, 2011).

As I will be discussing in subsequent chapters, there are outlets available to help calm the storm; to facilitate the checks and balances of our neuroendocrine system. Going back to Todd, how can he begin to move away from his disempowered position, being caught between his wife and son and disapproved of by both? Todd needed to focus first on his own body. Awareness of the tension in his chest, tightness in his jaw, shallowness in his breathing was a first step toward refocusing his attention on things he could influence, behaviors within his control.

In the middle of a crisis it is tremendously difficult to turn attention toward the body. Running from danger does not create space to focus on breathing. If under threat, I will be breathing short, shallow breaths, and that's the way it should be. I will need the adrenalin for energy to respond to the threat. However, long-term threat and prolonged stress require redirecting our focus from the threat itself to our response to the threat. With prolonged emotional threat, our bodies stay on alert, creating risk for physical and emotional harm. Todd also needed choice about how he interpreted his situation and how he responded.

Yes, the way my child is going, he may not finish high school, and his verbal abuse is hurting me greatly...AND I have a choice in how I interpret the situation and in how I respond. My mentally ill son may be sleeping in the bushes and be in physical danger, AND I have a choice in how I interpret the situation and in how I respond. My adult child may still be in my basement with no signs of motivation to move forward, AND I have a choice in how I interpret the situation and in how I respond.

I realize how difficult it is to talk about choice when consumed by worry about children. Perceived stress is as powerful as real stress. When there is an opportunity to reflect on how we are interpreting a situation or interaction, when we can approach a situation in an emotionally regulated way, when we can open ourselves to different perspectives then, to some extent, we can alter allostatic load and bring our system back to allostatis. Allostatis is balance. We want balance and perspective as much of the time as possible. Better for the mind, better for the body, and better for our relationships.

Todd's defense to the emotional pain he was experiencing flattened his sense of vitality and focus. Once a well-respected leader of his work team in a marketing firm, he now accepted the very minimum of performance from himself. Although he utilized one positive self-focus, maintaining a key role in the local Rotary club, all other areas of his life were diminished and overridden by his family situation. His fears were immense and many: the safety of his acting-out son, the uncertainty of his son's future, inability to forecast his son's emotional survival outside the home, anger at his son's treatment of him, guilt about his own anger, the sense of aloneness in his relationship with his wife, uncertainty about their future together, and so on.

The first substantial change came as Todd began to accept that he had little control regarding his son's attitude and behavior. His son was entering his senior year. His oppositional behavior was impenetrable at that specific time. Todd and his wife were not attuned to each other when they were in disagreement or conflict. His extensive efforts to provide a positive path for his son had come to naught. This was the time for a new perspective.

Todd interpreted his family situation as evidence of his inadequate parenting and his inadequacy as a husband. Along with that interpretation came guilt and helplessness. No amount of "trying" to parent well was helping his situation with his son or with his wife. He also experienced his son's abusive language as evidence that Jeffrey hated him, and this elicited great distress and sadness.

Focusing his attention on that interpretation negatively influenced Todd's ability to create choice, driving him into a restricted and stagnant state. The part of the brain that detects threat (the amygdala) has strong connections to the thinking part of the brain (the prefrontal cortex). Negative feelings can overwhelm more rational thought processes, influencing our assessment, judgment, and problem-solving abilities.

Change will require widening not only Todd's interpretation but also his tolerance for emotionally painful experiences. One theory of depression is that the depressed brain is unable to change in response to experience (Siegel, 2010d). The wider our window of tolerance, the more receptive instead of reactive we can be to the situations and experiences in our lives. As our window of tolerance widens and our experience changes from panic or depression to a calmer, clearer perspective on the situation, our brain changes as a result of that changed experience.

So for Todd, it becomes essential to his health and productivity in life to understand that his son's abusive treatment and oppositional behavior need to be addressed on a moment-to-moment basis. Todd cannot predict the future, and any interpretation of the meaning of Jeffrey's behavior is a guess, and our guesses usually lean on the catastrophic side.

Todd's issues with his wife are most likely multi-layered and will not, according to his own sense of things, be addressed until his son leaves the house. Progress for Todd would be to stay in a middle ground, somewhere between panic and disengagement, chaos and rigidity, despair and false hope, and make conscious choices how and where to focus his attention. If this is possible he may be able to avoid a sense of helplessness and increase his receptivity to other perspectives of this stressful situation. He may be able to accept what he can and cannot do and develop positive supports that exist for him in the present moment.

The goal is to acknowledge negative emotional states without being taken over by them, to see things as they presently are, rather than the way we think they should be, and to avoid assigning meanings that only serve to escalate distress. A most common interpretation made by a parent of a non-thriving child's behavior or situation is that the deficit or dysfunction in the child is due to "failed parenting." As I stated in the preface, this book is not about inadequate parenting. It is about parental survival in the face of difficult stressors.

As a psychologist, I am quite aware of the crucial effect of early childhood experiences and the connection between early parent-child attachment styles and adult deficits in interpersonal functioning. However, those of you reading this book are doing what you know how to do as parents and have perhaps become exhausted and weary on the emotionally rugged road. Opening to multiple perspectives and focusing attention on the choices available in the present moment can calm the inner turmoil at least enough to gain a degree of energy and vitality - enough to tolerate the high emotional arousal of the situation while attending to a prolonged and dangerous stress response. This is resilience.

LEARNED HELPLESSNESS

Martin Seligman, while studying the conditioning of dogs, developed the concept of learned helplessness. Learned helplessness identifies the psychological effect when an individual perceives he has no control over the outcome of a situation. Studies have connected learned helplessness with depression and related mental illnesses (Seligman 1967). Once learned, it appears that the state of learned helplessness is difficult to reverse.

Interesting studies have been conducted on the effects of learned helplessness. One particular study compared two groups of student volunteers who were all exposed to loud noise while each sat in a small room. The students in the first group, by experimenting with equipment in the room, each discovered that the noise level could be controlled by adjusting a lever. The second group, no matter what they tried, could not control the noise level.

The second part of the study involved putting both groups back in rooms with loud noise. This time, however, both groups were in rooms where the noise could be easily controlled by experimenting. As it turned out, the first group who had been able to control the noise in the first situation easily found the way to control noise the second time. However, the group that had no control over the noise level in the first situation was far more passive and didn't even try to find a way to control the noise in the second part of the study. (Abramson et. al.)

The conclusion: If individuals expect their behavior to have no affect on the outcome of a situation, the likelihood of responding with clarity, assertiveness, or motivation will be lessened. A horrifying example lies in the account of American soldiers opening the gates of Nazi concentration camps, only to be met with hesitant movements by the prisoners. We can see the same phenomenon in the child of an abusive parent who will not tell the truth about that parent because, in the child's experience, telling the truth will not change the situation (and will perhaps make it worse). And parents, who have tried so hard with little success, are vulnerable to experience themselves as helpless to change their heartbreaking parental situations.

Further results from the noise study concluded (through the use of pre and post personality tests) that students coming into the study with a strong externalized locus of control (the belief that the circumstances in my life are largely controlled by external factors) were more vulnerable to learned helplessness. Those coming into the study with a strong internalized locus of control (the belief that the situations in my life are largely in my control) were less likely to give up or feel helpless.

So the belief that your actions have an impact on the outcome of events in your life (a strong internal locus of control) increases proactive behaviors such as problem solving and perseverance. The outcome of the study also found that students who had no control over noise, as a group, performed poorer on simple mental tasks given at the end of the study. When we feel out of control of the circumstances in our lives, the stress response that accompanies that position makes us more vulnerable to depression and to reduced mental clarity. Although with non-thriving children, we may not have control over many circumstances, it is vitally important to identify areas of life of which we can take control.

Depression can be a consequence of experiencing life situations as out of one's control. The more we experience learned helplessness, the higher the risk of depression. And the greater the depression, the less control we feel. It's that loop. So experiences that lead us to feel helpless, to view life events as subject to external circumstances, not only increase the risk of depression but also reduce our ability to problem solve with clarity and focus. There is a connection between learned helplessness and the risk of depression which is exacerbated by an external locus of control.

I was struck by an article in the Seattle Times describing one family's struggle raising a mentally ill son. These parents had tried their best with their son Doug, supporting his eight year college attempt, purchasing a mobile home for him, and enlisting the support of mental health professionals. Their son disappeared at times, had delusional thoughts, and could not hold a menial job. What struck me about the article was the following statement by the young man's father: "We finally came to the conclusion we couldn't change our son, but we changed the way we interacted with him which made life much better."(Seattle Times, 2/26/ 2012)

They took control of how they responded to him, really the only thing they could control. They reduced their experiences of helplessness by responding to their son in ways that reduced chaos and disruption in all of their lives. For example, when their son yelled at them, they would send him out of the room. "He'd go—and the room would settle." Seemingly small changes in their responses gave them a sense of control over their own emotional state, which can reduce the danger of learned helplessness.

Remember Sharon whose sons relentlessly sided with their father's accusations and abusive communication to her? She resorted to offering a gun to one of her sons, asking that he end her misery. Sharon needed a new perspective (to say the least). She was obsessed with defending herself to her verbally abusive and entitled sons, and that obsession spilled out into other relationships. She and I rehearsed assertive statements that were very difficult for her given the high emotional arousal of her defensiveness.

However, she began to experience some success. Lines such as "I'm sorry you feel that way" (implying no guilt), "I won't have a conversation with you when you are talking to me that way" (ending the abuse by hanging up the phone) were helpful. Defining some rules of engagement also worked well: don't beg, don't repeat yourself, don't keep calling when they hang up on you, move on, move forward, seek support, find distractions that are meaningful to you, and so on.

Sharon began to feel more control of her own emotional response. Don't forget, the brain changing as a result of experience. Our experiences can change our brains. As she began to assert herself and reduce her defensive behavior, it became easier for her to stay in a more emotionally regulated place.

She still cries often, feels lonely in her home, and experiences losing "everything important to me." However, she has made a decision to sell her home (which has enraged her sons even though they are both in college) because it feels empty and lonely there.

She has decided to travel more with a friend (she used to worry that her children would accuse her of being selfish to spend so much money on herself) and to view her current situation with the perspective that it may not be permanent.

She has given herself permission to take care of herself while her sons (hopefully) grow up. She has found some areas within the stressful situation where she can take control over her situation and, therefore, her life. As she takes more control over the areas she *can* control, she reduces her stance of helplessness. And, you know how the loop works. The more she feels in control of her own emotional responses, the less risk of helplessness and depression and, therefore, she becomes a more hardy support for her sons.

Changing the focus of attention away from defensiveness, anger, self-blame, guilt, and hopelessness has given Sharon some space to breathe. And that is what she is looking for—a space to breathe and to have her own life, while, at the same time, experiencing great hurt and pain regarding her children. We cannot hope or expect that she will eliminate the pain, but experiencing the choice of where to put her attention will change the outcome for her.

Yes, the brain changes as an outcome of experience. Isn't that amazing! Experience activates neural firing, which in turn leads to the production of proteins that enable new connections to be made among neurons. (Siegel, 2010e) This is the process of neuroplasticity. "Neuro" refers to the nerve cells in our brains and nervous systems, and "plastic" means changeable or modifiable.

Parents involved with difficult or non-thriving children can get stuck in their emotional and physical responses to stressful, hurtful, or heartbreaking situations. The goal is to increase flexibility, widen the window of tolerance, avoid prolonged stress in the body, and expand the areas of life of which you are in control. All of these things will decrease the possibility of depression and hopelessness. As we practice new responses to difficult situations, the areas of the brain needed to continue those new responses expand, and we become increasingly more adept at initiating those stress-reducing responses.

In 2000, neuroscientist Eleanor Maguire of University College London carried out a study involving London cabdrivers. Unlike in the United States, London cabdrivers spend up to three years learning the difficult labyrinth of streets running throughout the city. They are required to pass an examination called "The Knowledge" which tests their ability to quickly navigate through the streets of London.

The hippocampus is a part of the brain important in spatial learning and memory, something cab drivers actively engage in all day long, learning the streets and by-ways of London. Brain scans determined that among these London cabdrivers who studied for years to pass the exam, the hippocampus was significantly larger than in people who were not involved in such learning. The point here is that engaging actively and with attention builds new neuropathways. The more a part of the brain is used, the more effective it can be. Not so different than using a muscle.

What new neuropathways do we want to create for dealing with heartbreak parenting situations? We want our experiences to empower us, not defeat us. We want to intentionally choose where to focus our attention. We want to invest in activities that engage us, providing meaningful distraction and creating avenues of control. Engaging actively and with attention promotes new neuropathways. We want those pathways to provide outlets for frustration, anger, fear, dread and all those incredibly difficult emotions that accompany the heartbreak of our children's situations.

The goal for struggling parents is to help their children reduce suffering and be happy in their lives. Parents also want and need to calm the storm, to build new perspectives, and find meaningful avenues to their own growth and well-being. To focus attention on reducing their *own_*stress *as a priority* is often part of the paradigm change, meaning very difficult to accomplish. Self-focus will enhance a parent's ability to be present and effective as a resource for their children. This is often a new perspective for a parent who is consumed by the stress surrounding their children's situations. This new perspective, however, can be the impetus for the redirection of attention and energy, thereby reducing the risks associated with holding prolonged stress without available outlets or supports.

We calm the storm, and make ourselves more resourceful and effective with non-thriving children by nurturing the part of our own lives that can be separate from the intensity of overwhelmingly negative feelings. We work toward building a sense of control over meaningful areas of our own lives and practice self-soothing behaviors that reduce the damaging effects of prolonged stress.

We find ways to keep moving to avoid the dangerous loop of depression. We calm the storm by staying aware that we have a choice in how we interpret situations and in how we respond. We calm the storm by creating positive experiences and new perspectives in the midst of painful emotional experiences. All of this increases our effectiveness in dealing with difficult situations. Although this is a paradigm change in thinking, our goal remains the same; to be the most effective, emotionally regulated resource for our children.

CHAPTER 6

Finding Your Neutral

WHEN WE FEEL under threat, frustrated, helpless, hopeless, or fearful, our ability to focus and problem-solve will be diminished and our perspective jeopardized. We will be at risk of either becoming overly rigid (Laura not answering her schizophrenic son's calls for fear she would lose her boundaries) or overwhelmed and out of control (Sharon offering the gun to her son to just "put me out of my misery.") Under these conditions, the stress response will be activated and openness to new ways of looking at things will be restricted.

Claudia, whose son is somewhere on his own with a drug and drinking problem, dreads the evening phone call from her son who offers her no assurance that he is safe and sober. And, Todd each evening on his drive home anticipates the conflict between his son and wife and how he will be squarely and unsuccessfully in the middle as he walks through the door. For both of these parents, the anticipation of a stressful situation consumes their day.

To repeat, this book does not directly address parenting skills. Rather, we are interested in vital skills for parents to reduce their stress, feel a sense of control, think clearly, be able to respond to stressful situations receptively rather than reactively, and to intentionally choose where to focus attention. The stakes are high because prolonged stress has such damaging physiological and psychological impact. One powerful tool that offers help in all of these areas is the practice of mindfulness meditation.

Hearing a yoga teacher ask her class to "find your neutral" caught my attention. First, I wasn't really sure where my neutral was, let alone how to find it. Eventually I realized that finding neutral in your body is like allostasis in the hormonal system—a balanced place that keeps the system vibrant and calm at the same time; a place where the autonomic nervous system is operating optimally. From neutral you can shift to any available gear. From neutral you have choice. I saw a clear analogy between the practice of finding neutral and the practice of mindfulness meditation.

According to Jon Kabat-Zinn, founding director of the Stress Reduction Clinic and the Center for Mindfulness in Medicine at University of Massachusetts, "mindfulness is awareness, cultivated by paying attention in a sustained and particular way: on purpose, in the present moment, and non-judgmentally." (Kabat-Zinn, 2012a) It is the non-judgmental concept that seems to be so difficult. When things feel out of control in our lives or when they are not going the way we want them to go, our self-judgment—or the judgment of others—can be harsh.

A new patient, Veronica, while discussing her daughter's self-destructive behavior, said to me "I wake up at night thinking how stupid I have been for rescuing her and giving her one more chance over and over again, while she's been lying to me about everything." Veronica's anger was now getting in her way; this anger had taken front and center stage as a topic of her middle of the night worry.

Veronica needed a way to calm the HPA loop which she was fueling with self- anger as well as with anger at her daughter. Her anger was understandable but unproductive and harmful. She would obviously benefit from a practice that would help her feel more centered, have more clarity, and be more receptive to available options. If she was not consumed by her anger and self-judgment, she could more effectively move forward with the difficult and painful situation she experienced with her daughter. She needed to find access to a neutral state of being. Although finding this neutral state does not solve the situational problem, nor does it take away the pain, it does help create a sense of emotional balance and the ability to reflect with clarity before reacting.

Mindfulness is one form of meditation, and it has roots that are deep and wide. Today it is connected more to general well-being than to any particular religious practice. From Buddhist meditation practices to Catholic centering prayer, from Marine fitness programs to neuroscience, mindfulness has empirically and clinically been shown to provide an individual with an increased capacity to direct attention, to reduce judgment or negative thinking and to approach problems from a receptive rather than reactive position; all tools that help parents calm the storm and turn off the stress response.

What is the importance of facilitating a state of receptivity rather than reactivity? Of course there are situations that require us to be reactive, and sometimes quickly reactive. As parents, we certainly know those situations. However, responding to the ongoing stressful experiences that involve our children requires us to be fully present with our own bodily reactions and stay attentive and clear thinking at the same time. Paying attention to their needs *and* our needs, in tandem, requires our full presence, both to ourselves and to the other person. When the alarm goes off in our heads, it sets in place all those chemical and physiological processes that are activated by stress and which encumbers our ability to choose where to put our attention.

Veronica, consumed with anger at herself and her daughter, serves as an example of the debilitating, all encompassing reactions that can occur when we become overwhelmed and unable to redirect our attention to self-care. Veronica was worried about her adult daughter who had, once again, walked out of a drug rehab program. She received news that her daughter had returned to living with a drug abusing boyfriend, and was refusing to communicate with family.

On hearing this news about her daughter, Veronica went to bed for a week, not showering, brushing her teeth, or working. These were behaviors uncharacteristic of this woman. Her accumulated worry and sense of helplessness to protect her daughter and shame about her daughter's very public, self-destructive behavior had impaired her ability to focus on her own body and her own needs. She had rendered herself helpless, which was creating a negative spiral of depression, followed by an increased sense of helplessness: none of which helped her daughter and put her at risk physically and mentally. She could only break that dangerous spiral by redirecting her focus to the areas of her life where she could take control: getting out of bed, showering, working and focusing on both her husband and other children in the family. Interrupting the downward spiral required her to choose where to direct her focus. As a patient said to me, "This is a hell of a difficult thing to do." Yes, it is.

The practice of mindfulness involves not so much a method or technique as a way of being or "a way of seeing." (Segal et.al. 2002) It is a way of becoming more aware and more absorbed in our focus and attention. I see the practice of mindfulness as a way to change our perspective on what we see, what we feel, and what we think. It is also a way of moving our locus of control from external to internal by taking control of where we focus our attention. Mindfulness practice helps us be present without judgment and without reactivity. From that perspective, we increase our ability to recognize and acknowledge a feeling without being consumed by it. Veronica, in the downward spiral, was indeed consumed by her emotions.

The feelings connected to our children's struggles, or to our difficult relationships with our children, are pervasive and intense. Learning to stay aware of difficult feelings without being consumed by them becomes an important skill of well-being. Kabot-Zinn states, "...You may discover that cultivating mindfulness has a way of giving your life back to yourself..." (Kabat-Zinn, 2012b) And for parents with the preoccupying stress of non-thriving or problematic children, this is a much needed tool.

One of the benefits of mindfulness is emotional balance; staying emotionally alive and yet not overwhelmed by the intensity of negative emotions. This is neutral. This is allostasis. This is the two branches of the autonomic nervous system working optimally. Worry about our children is often future-focused. "Yes, I'm concerned and upset about the way my son talks to me, but I also worry about how he will treat women in his life. Will he ever have a successful relationship?" If mindfulness training can yield an increased ability to be in the present moment, then we can focus on bodily and emotional responses to present experiences with future concerns as a background rather than the main, preoccupying event.

As of 2001, only 28 scientific papers on mindfulness had been published. Within the last decade, however, over 400 scientific articles have been published yearly. (Mindful, 2013) The plethora of studies conducted at major universities throughout the world offer us consistent documentation of lasting decreases in anxiety, helplessness, and depression, and documentation of increases in stress management skills through the practice of mindfulness. (Hofmann, et.al. 2010a) The literature yields reports of greater relaxation and an increase in energy and enthusiasm for life.

Even the United States Marine Corps is studying the effectiveness of mindfulness practices. A pilot study, designed by former U.S. Army captain and Georgetown University professor Elizabeth Stanley, drew on scientific research indicating that regular meditation reduces depression, boosts memory and the immune system, and "grows the parts of the brain responsible for memory and emotional regulation." In Stanley's pilot study, a group of Marines practiced mindfulness 12 minutes a day for eight weeks. The test results concluded that the Marines who practiced mindfulness had better sleep, improved athletic performance, and higher scores on emotional and cognitive evaluations than Marines who did not participate in the study. (Watson, 2013) Improving sleep and cognitive functioning and increasing the ability to regulate emotions are valuable outcomes in dealing with the ongoing worries, concerns, and frustrations of stressed parents.

In addition, current literature from controlled studies offers consistent conclusions that mindfulness practices increase our ability to cope more effectively with short-term and long-term stressful situations. (Hozel, et.al. 2010) That certainly is a tool badly needed by parents who experience chronic stress and worry.

Dr. Shanida Naturaja, author of _The Blissful Brain_, (Nataraja, 2008a) states that mindfulness practice can bring about calmness, still brain chatter and help us shift toward a right brain mode, which is the mode responsible primarily for modulation of emotion. Dr. Naturaja, goes further to state that mindfulness practices create changes in our brains. These changes are created by the activation of the parasympathetic nervous system, which is the system in the brain, as discussed earlier, that promotes relaxation. As different neural and hormonal triggers come into place, the sympathetic nervous system, which is the system responsible for arousal, becomes activated, producing an increase in mental clarity and alertness.

Mindfulness practices result in positive changes in breathing rate, heart rate, blood pressure, cognition and mood. (Hofmann, et.al. 2010) Contrary to what we might assume, it does not take years of mindfulness practice to make significant differences in how we feel and function. Dr. Fadel Zeidan, a researcher at Wake Forest University School of Medicine, performed a well-designed experiment comparing participants who had received 4 twenty minute mindfulness training sessions to participants in a control group who had listened to a reading of the Hobbit. The mindfulness trained group performed ten times better on a test that measured the ability to sustain focus while holding other information in mind. (Zeidan, et.al. 2010)

This becomes particularly essential when the "other information" is overwhelming, frightening and seemingly out of our direct control and involves our children and our relationship with them. Sustained focus facilitates clear thinking, helps us pause before we react, problem solve better, and access options more readily. These are valuable skills, or states of being, that will enhance our capacity to endure the emotional pain of dealing with non-thriving children without being overwhelmed or, as my patient Claudia states, "waking each morning in a state of dread."

In a very short period of time, mindfulness practices can help us regulate emotions so we can think clearly and perform better cognitively. When Rita offered the gun to her son, she was not thinking clearly or rationally. She needed to find her neutral. She badly needed a pause between her intense feelings and her behavior. Mindfulness practices facilitate these states of being.

In the study by Zeidan, participants were tested in stressful situations. Mindfulness trained participants performed better under stress than the control group. My patient who asked me "What am I supposed to do?" will want to perform as well as he can under the stress of dealing with a difficult situation with his child. He will want to be able to focus on his work and on his life, while dealing with stress in the most non-reactive way possible. That is what he is "supposed to do." Mindfulness practices can help toward that goal.

Dr. Zeidan, the lead researcher of this study, states as a summary; "It goes to show that the mind is, in fact, easily changeable and highly influenced, especially by mindfulness." He goes on to say, "…the meditater's first benefits may be associated with increasing the ability to sustain attention." To be able to choose where we focus our attention is a worthwhile benefit when facing situations that cause us to "lose our minds." Dan Siegel puts it this way: "Creating a hub of awareness enables us to acknowledge troubling states without being taken over by them and to see things as they are rather than being constrained by our expectations of how they 'should be'." (Siegel, 2010f) When operating from a "hub of awareness" there are many spokes of reactions and behaviors from which to choose. The "hub" is like neutral; an emotional and physical state from which we can choose our interpretations and our responses to difficult situations.

I recently saw a documentary film about a boy named Sam who is one of a very few children suffering from Progeria, a very rare and devastating genetic condition involving accelerated aging. (Fine, 2013) Statements made by Sam's mother and father particularly caught my attention. Both expressed the choice they had made not to accept the prognosis that there was no available treatment, no research, no attention being directed at this condition because of the small number of children affected (less than 300 worldwide.) Sam's parents, both physicians, chose to research and test a drug treatment, and against many obstacles, they did. Even though this treatment did not save their son, Sam's mother states, "I'm not angry. It's counterproductive. I don't wallow in 'this isn't fair. It isn't worth it." Sam's father speaks of the need to take in the joyful moments. They are all we have. Sam's parents were able to choose how to look at their situation and how to respond.

Meditation is a tool that brings us into the present moment to experience it with full attention. We will enhance a sense of control and begin an emotional upward spiral as we increase our ability to take in the moments and to be able to think clearly and respond as non-reactively as possible. Choosing to interpret an event or situation without catastrophic thinking, and to have practiced skills to remain mentally and physically calm enough to avoid activating the HPA feedback loop are benefits of mindfulness training.

The goal is not to eliminate our built-in stress-response. That would be impossible and dangerous. The objective is to be able to turn it off when its continuous activation is dangerous to our health. Don't forget the "too much, too little principle." The stress response is incredible protection to deal with the lions that chase us. But if we can't turn the response off, we suffer and lose capacity.

Sharon needed ways to turn off the stress response before she went to the garage to get the gun. Todd needed that skill to be able to attend to his work while dealing with the oppositional behavior of his son and the blame from his wife. Barbara needed that skill when she realized her health was in jeopardy and that she needed to pay attention to her body and her own personal and professional goals.

David Creswell has worked with the difficult problem of loneliness in the elderly population. Many types of interventions have been tried with very little, if any, success. Bringing the elderly together for activities or creating environments that could promote friendships have failed to impact loneliness according to Creswell. However, when he provided training in Mindfulness Based Stress Reduction (MBSR), loneliness diminished. This MBSR training consisted of an eight-week program that emphasized focused awareness and experiences to help participants become grounded in the present moment. (Creswell, et.al. 2012)

Rick Hanson, PhD, author of _Buddha's Brain_, describes some of the benefits of regular meditation. (Hanson 2009). He includes in his lengthy list of positive outcomes the following benefits: **decreases** in stress-related cortisol, insomnia, autoimmune illnesses, falling back into depression, general emotional distress, anxiety and **increases** in immune system factors, self-understanding, and general well-being. This quite significant list and much more can be found consistently in a multitude of studies.

Dr. Hanson states that regular meditation increases gray matter in the insula (a part of the brain associated with self-awareness and empathy), in the hippocampus (associated with calming the amygdala and the production of stress hormones in the body), and in the prefrontal cortex which supports executive functions such as decision making and problem solving.

As discussed in earlier chapters, when we are stressed, we secrete adrenalin and cortisol into our bodies, supplying energy to deal with crisis. With prolonged stress responses, stress hormones become elevated, not just to respond to a crisis, but spike even in the face of minor stresses.

High levels of stress hormones in the body not only create risk for many physical diseases and illness but can be toxic to the brain and can interfere with neural tissue. (Siegel, 2010g) And, more relevant to the situation of heartbreak parenting, chronically elevated stress hormones sensitize limbic reactivity, which means that even minor stresses become more difficult to address and emotional balance in dealing with these situations becomes more difficult to achieve.

Remember Veronica who went to bed for days without attending to even the most basic of daily functioning because she had discovered once again that her daughter had lied to her and was continuing a high risk life style? Work tasks, personal hygiene, attention to family, phone calls from friends all became too difficult to handle. She had lost emotional balance. Stress hormones, elevated by her chronic worry and anger regarding her daughter's situation, had over- sensitized her limbic system. Previously non-stressful activities had become overwhelming.

A very effective tool for Veronica was learning to focus on her breathing in a sustained and intentional way. Focused breathing is often used as a vehicle for meditation and mindfulness. She was learning to use an anti-anxiety tool that put her more in control of her emotional responses. That tool helped her to problem solve and choose her responses.

A study published in the journal Pediatrics (Dykens, 2014) reports the results of placing 243 mothers of children with disabilities randomly into either a Mindfulness-Based Stress Reduction

(MBSR) group or a Positive Adult Development (positive psychology practice) group. Eighty-five percent of this cohort of women had significantly elevated stress. Forty-eight percent were clinically depressed and forty-one percent had anxiety disorders. Both groups met once a week for 1.5 hours for 6 weeks.

Results of the study showed significant reduction in stress, depression and anxiety, improved sleep and life satisfaction in both groups. Mothers in the MBSR groups had greater improvements in anxiety, depression, sleep and well-being. This study addressed the need to attend to the mental health of mothers living with the elevated stress factors of raising children with disabilities and the positive result of mindfulness practices for this community of mothers.

And a final encouraging study, in my hope of being persuasive regarding the benefits of meditation and mindfulness practices, involves telomere length (the end caps to our chromosomes that have been linked to aging at a cellular level). Practicing meditation for three months has been shown to preserve telomere length. Increased mind wandering, meaning less control of where we direct our attention, has been associated with shortened telomeres. We want as much control over our response to stress as we can get, and mindfulness/meditation practices have been shown to increase the control we have in directing our attention and awareness and perhaps to slow down the aging process at a cellular level.

Mindfulness helps create the capacity for emotional balance, which makes it easier to acknowledge a feeling without being consumed by it. The beleaguered feeling, the fear, the stress, the preoccupation with a child who is not thriving, suffering or behaving abusively or self-destructively; these feelings throw us out of emotional balance. Being able to self-soothe during emotional chaos, maintaining a modicum of perspective and present-moment centeredness can turn off the signal that informs the limbic system that we're in crisis and need stress hormones to cope.

Back again to Sharon who offered her son a gun to "just end it once and for all." Sharon needed a way to self-soothe during the crisis. Her meltdown was the result of a lack of emotional balance. In this out of balance state we are more likely to move toward one of two extremes. Either we experience a state of excessive emotional arousal and a sense of out-of-control (Sharon and her gun) or we move toward a rigid, low arousal state of depression or despair (Veronica and her non-functioning meltdown.)

Sharon benefited from learning to more accurately assign meaning to her son's behavior. He didn't hate her. She wasn't a bad parent. He was manipulative, as are many teenagers given the opportunity. He was also abusive in his language to her and highly influenced by his father, something Sharon realized but couldn't tap into while in such a high arousal state. You can see how the benefit of mental clarity and emotional regulation could create a shift in Sharon's ability to respond.

For Sharon, learning to stay centered involved reaching out to friends, not to share these experiences (because she already did too much of that) but to focus on something, anything, other than the difficult and draining behaviors of her children. She learned that she could choose where to focus her energy. Her children were not in charge of that. Increased activities with friends who were energized and stable, attention to breathing while feeling the onslaught of her son's accusations, mindfulness practices, setting boundaries for what she will tolerate, attending again to aerobic exercise, and beginning classes at a local college to enhance job skills helped Sharon keep a more open and flexible perspective and reduced her despair while increasing her focus on her own life.

As Sharon increased her ability to regulate emotional states, she could more effectively respond to her children's abusive language without "crumbling inside." Their behavior hasn't much changed, but her sense of threat and guilt has been reduced. She spends more energy now on what she can control and is working on accepting the way things are for now. Change in her adult children will have to take its own course, but her ability to focus on self-care does not depend on changes in them.

Gaining the ability to self-regulate increases our flexibility in responding to conflict and distressful situations. Emotional regulation is enhanced by self-soothing practices such as focused breathing and mindfulness practices, both of which facilitate the ability to pause and become fully aware of the situation in the moment and to choose how to respond.

When we are centered and able to self-regulate, our brain more fully utilizes our middle prefrontal region, a part of the brain that has evolved only in humans. This part of the brain has regulatory functions that enable us to have that all-so-important pause before we respond. "A pause is a suspension of activity, a time of temporary disengagement when we are no longer moving toward any goal." (Brach, 2012) Keeping this part of the brain turned on is essential in dealing with stress.

My husband and I, and occasionally my daughters, are fans of our local football team, the Seattle Seahawks. I noticed during a recent game how many times the announcers commented on the wide stance of the sensational running back Marshawn Lynch. He could not be taken down because he was so centered to the ground, with feet wide apart, never off balance. He could push forward for additional yards because his centeredness let him withstand the assault. Self-regulation is somewhat like "feet wide apart", not taken down by the distress, able to navigate through situations because of the ability to pause long enough to become fully aware and to choose what meaning to assign a situation and how best to respond. That is centeredness; that is "feet wide apart".

There is an abundance of literature, including classes, books, tapes, apps and retreats that guide the novice into mindfulness practices. It is not difficult to get started. Just begin by taking a small amount of time to pause and notice where you are choosing to put your attention. Many guides for beginning mindfulness practices suggest finding an anchor of some sort, an image, a word or using breath as a source of focus. Focusing on the breath can be an easy and helpful way to begin.

Just take a moment to notice if your breathing is shallow, going down only as far as your chest cavity, or if you inhale deeply and into your diaphragm. Notice the air coming in through your nose and out through your mouth. When you exhale, put a slight sound to your breath which will increase your awareness of the smoothness or raggedness of your breathing. It is the long, slow exhale that informs your brain that everything is all right. Just allow yourself that pause. Focusing on breath is a common meditation practice and an easy way to get started.

The challenge will be to avoid judging your success at mindfulness practices. Stay aware of your judgmental self-talk. I have found myself saying, "I'm just not the meditating type. I'm too active, too restless for this." Becoming aware of my negative thinking was helpful and directed me toward walking meditations that are actually a lot easier for me. Finding a way to calm the often tumultuous, anxiety-producing chatter that captures and consumes our attention will reap great benefits in dealing with the stressful, fearful experience of parenting non-thriving children. Just begin by sitting and noticing. Keep in mind there are extensive resources and helpful guidance available.

Christopher K. Germer puts it so simply; "Mindfulness----has long been used to lessen the sting of life's difficulties." (Germer et.al. 2005) Mindfulness research has consistently documented reports from participants of lasting decreases in negative emotions and lasting increases in stress management skills. The ability to relax and have greater energy and enthusiasm for life and the increased ability to cope effectively with short-term and long-term stressful situations is what most struggling parents are looking for.

We are interested in answers to my patient's question "What am I supposed to do?" In part, the answer involves how to stay well, how to be in charge in as many areas of your life as possible, how to turn off the stress response when it becomes chronic and long term and jeopardizes mental and physical health. Mindfulness is one practice that has proven to be responsive to all of those challenges.

John O'Donohue, in his beautiful book of Celtic wisdom, tells the story told to him about the wolf-spider. He compares the flexible, resilient mind to a wolf-spider's web. The wolf-spider would never construct its web between two hard objects such as rocks. If it did, the web would be destroyed easily by the winds and weather that surely would come. The wolf-spider instinctively lays out its web between two blades of grass that bend and flex against the strength of the wind. As the flexible blades of grass lower into the wind, so does the delicate web. When the wind passes, the web "comes back up and finds its point of balance and equilibrium again." (O'Donohue, et.al. 1997) This is the balancing act of the resilient mind. This is the mind in neutral, intentionally deciding where to put its focus. Mindfulness is a tool, a practice that assists us to claim this resiliency.

CHAPTER 7

Social Affiliation

HERE IS A fascinating study result: Social interaction has a powerful impact on neurogenesis, which means the birth of new neurons. Elizabeth Gould speculates from her study results (Stranahan, et.al.) that social support "blunted the reactivity" of the HPA axis (remember how that axis can get sensitized and over reactive?) and kept the stress hormones from interfering with growth of new neurons. So could social support help us turn down our reactivity to the events in our lives? Could it help us at a cellular level to support growth of new neurons that could be influential in memory and learning functions? And, most significantly to our topic, could social support reduce the damaging physiological and psychological effects of prolonged stress which we know is plentiful for parents of non-thriving, struggling or difficult children?

Social support simply means having people in our lives that are meaningful to us and provide needed resources. Those resources might consist of information exchanged, a sense of belonging, emotional support or intimacy. Social support might come from being associated with a larger organization, an intimate group of friends or a single confidant.

In her presentation at Osher Center for Integrative Medicine, Dr. Elissa Epel, PhD discusses the role of stress in gene expression. (Epel, 2012) To the question, "Can we change our genes?" Dr. Epel explains that we cannot change our genes, but we can influence the expression of our genes. Stress can promote inflammation and inflammation can turn on gene expression, making us more vulnerable to disease. But here is the really fascinating part: Apparently loneliness also can alter gene expression. "..genes can be activated or inhibited by signals circulating in the body, such as hormones." (Twyman, 2003) We know that stress hormones can be activated not only by stress, but perhaps also by the condition of loneliness and isolation.

Social support is a strong and consistent predictor of health outcomes, and social isolation predicts increased morbidity and mortality. Dr. Berkman from Yale School of Medicine states, "There is now a substantial body of evidence that indicates that the extent to which social relationships are strong and supportive is related to the health of individuals." (Berkman, 1995)

The literature demonstrates the role of social support as a protective factor against the damaging effects of chronic stress. For example, one study concluded that greater quality of social support is associated with lower cortisol concentrations in women with metastatic breast cancer. Lower cortisol means healthier neuroendocrine functioning. (Turner-Cobb et.al. 2000)

A study conducted by House, Landis, and Umberson concluded that, for the same illness, people with the fewest social connections have about two-and-a-half times as much chance of dying as those with the most social connections. (House, et.al. 1988) Sapolsky states, "the fewer social relationships a person has, the shorter his or her life expectancy, and the worse the impact of various infectious diseases." (Sapolsky, 1994f)

Dr. Elizabeth Blackburn is a Nobel Prize winner for her research on telomeres. She studied mothers of children with disabilities who had been meeting together on a regular basis to support each other and share their emotional and personal experiences while raising children with special needs. Blackburn found that the length of telomeres measured in these women was directly related to not only the amount of stress, but also to the number of years the stress had continued. (Bredar, 2008b)

Dr. Epel also took interest in this group of women, looking to find a connection between women undergoing intensely stressful situations who had ongoing social support and the effectiveness of the enzyme telomerase (see stress response chapter) which can repair damage to the telomere. She concluded that social affiliation can stimulate the healing effect of the telomerase enzyme, repairing damage and preventing the fraying of the telomeres that ultimately speeds the death of the cell. Now this is an incredible finding. As discussed in early chapters, the fraying of telomeres (the end caps of our chromosomes) leads to the death of a cell; the aging process. The enzyme telomerase, which can apparently, under certain circumstances, repair and prevent damage to telomeres, was facilitated by social affiliation. So, perhaps social affiliation staves off the death of our cells.

A study published in the New England Journal of Medicine involved bereaved parents of Israeli soldiers killed in the Lebanese War. (Leval, et.al. 1988) This 10-year study concluded that the loss of a child did not increase the mortality of the parents in general. However, the parents who had, previous to their child's death, either divorced or were widowed had higher mortality rates than those who had a spouse. This conclusion certainly points to the protective factor of social support.

Conclusions from a study of Three Mile Island residents after the nuclear accident seem relevant to the on-going stress of difficult parenting issues. These researchers found that residents who had moderate or high levels of social support were better able to cope with and adapt to stress than were residents without social support. Higher levels of social support were associated with fewer psychological and behavioral symptoms resulting from stress. (Fleming et.al. 1982)

If the stressor is by nature more or less continuous, as is true while struggling with issues concerning our children, social support does no better in ending stress or reducing arousal than any other protective factor. In other words, social support does help us cope, but, of course, it does not solve the problem. It does provide a protective factor, but our alarm button will be just as sensitized, our fears or frustration just as intense, even with good support from people who matter to us. However, protecting ourselves the best we can from the many risk factors associated with chronic stress provides us with more ability to be present and thrive in our own lives. Social support is a protective factor, not a solution to an often intense, on-going stressor.

In many ways, all of the above might be self-evident. It is better to have a friend than not. It is better to have a supportive partner than not. Belonging to a like-minded group or having supportive friends is a boost to self-esteem and in some ways an antidote to loneliness. Loneliness is associated with increases in stress factors that subject us to emotional and physical harm. Being with people who understand our situation and who perhaps share a similar situation helps decrease stress hormones in our bodies. We are social beings and benefit in numerous ways when we seek and sustain relationships that provide support.

Unless we have built-in social support systems or a personality structure that readily gravitates toward acquiring and sustaining social support, establishing and utilizing a network of people of like-mind is no simple task. However, it's important to know that it's important. Social support is not a luxury but a protective factor that helps us deal with overwhelming thoughts and feelings with regard to our children's well-being and/or the quality of our relationships with our children.

As discussed, research in the last 20 years indicates that strong and supportive social relationships are related to the health of individuals. For social support to be health-promoting and protective it must "provide both a sense of belonging and intimacy and must help people to be more competent and self-efficacious." (Berkman, 1995) I often hear from struggling parents that their friends do not understand and have no frame of reference for what they are experiencing. Their friends often give quick and easy advice which is out of touch with their struggles. Social support as a protective factor is not just having people around, but having people around who offer a greater sense of belonging to a community of sorts. Social support that makes a difference to general health and stress reduction is not easy to find, but it is worth seeking.

Run for Your Life

Or Walk or Bike or Spin or Just Move a Lot

REBECCA SUFFERS FROM depression. Her two adult children struggle with their own psychiatric issues and neither has the capacity or disposition to be of support. When her son treats her badly or inattentively Rebecca responds by retreating to the comfort of her house, her couch, her bed, or her T.V. Since she is retired and lives alone, this immobile life is available to her without much consequence from the outside world, but has significant consequence to her brain and body.

We often think of physical exercise as a source of muscle and endurance building, weight loss, and enhancement of physical health and appearance. All of these are significant effects, however, the benefits to the brain are even more fascinating and at least equally life enhancing. Our bodies are built to move, and yet the amount of movement needed to survive in modern times is minimal. As we have discussed earlier, the stress response signals our bodies to respond, to react in some way: run from that noise, lift up that car, run to the stove to turn off the burner, fix the problem. Psychological stress often does not lend itself to a physical solution. However, on-going physical exercise provides not only a reduction but also a prevention of the deleterious effects of prolonged stress, allowing the body an outlet for built-up, stress-related energy.

Dr. John J. Ratey explains, "In the body, physical activity lowers the resting tension of the muscles and thus interrupts the anxiety feedback loop to the brain. If the body is calm, the brain is less prone to worry." (Ratey, 2008c) He is talking about the HPA loop that we've been discussing. By working our muscles, we produce calming chemical reactions in the brain, and our bodies break down fat molecules to fuel the muscles. This process frees fatty acids in the bloodstream. This is a good thing because the freeing of fatty acids stimulates the concentration of tryptophan in the bloodstream. Tryptophan is used as a building block for serotonin which plays an important part in the regulation of learning, mood, and sleep.

Just allowing our bodies to move triggers the release of Gamma-Aminobutyric acid (GABA), the brain's major inhibitory neurotransmitter. GABA interrupts the HPA loop within the brain and produces a molecule that slows down hyper-aroused states. Studies support the idea that there is indeed a connection between how much you exercise and how anxious you feel. (Ratey 2008d)

The positive effects of exercise on mental clarity, mood, and stress reduction are clear in the research. But how does physical movement directly affect psychological states? The benefits of aerobic exercise have a neurochemical source. Exercise reduces the stress hormones (adrenalin and cortisol) and stimulates the production of endorphins, which are the body's natural painkillers and mood elevators.

As most exercisers have experienced, one of the positive effects of exercise is this increase in endorphins. Not only does exercise elevate endorphins, but it also regulates all of the neurotransmitters, such as dopamine and serotonin. Dopamine positively affects mood and helps us feel motivated and focused. Serotonin also has a positive effect on mood and helps counteract cortisol while under stress.

Anti-depressant medications act on these same neurotransmitters. A study done in 1999 at Duke University by James Blumenthal was designed to compare the effects of an anti-depressant medication (Zoloft) with the effects of exercise on subjects diagnosed with major depression. One group received the medication, one group exercised 30 minutes three times a week, and one group did both. Results of this study demonstrated that exercise was equally as effective as the medication. What an amazing conclusion; exercise can change brain chemistry just as well as medication. (Blumenthal, and Babyak, 1999)

The results of a six-month follow-up study, on the same subjects, were even more surprising. This study concluded that those who continued to exercise, but did not receive Zoloft, actually did *better* than the other two groups. This was another amazing conclusion. The researchers speculated about why the group that did both, exercised and took Zoloft, did not do as well in relieving depression as the group that just exercised. They point to the possibility that subjects who exercised as well as took medication credited their lowered depression to the effects of the medication instead of to their hard work at exercising. In other words, the subjects who did both lost the anti-depressing effects that occur when we successfully take control of a major area of our lives. Taking control of any significant area of our lives is, in itself, an anti-depressant behavior. (Babysk and Blumenthal, 2000)

The exercisers in Blumenthal's follow-up studies were motivated to exercise. They took control of that aspect of their lives. And taking that control may have accounted for the resulting conclusion that exercise did better at reducing depression than did exercise *and* medication. Two things were at play; physical exercise and taking control of something that mattered. Both can be anti-depressants.

The stress-response is remarkable in its complexity and protective functions. As we have seen over and over in earlier chapters, if we cannot turn on the stress-response or if we cannot turn it off we suffer. We need to recover from stress, to relax, to turn off the stress-response, to stop the HPA feedback loop. Not only does physical exercise "ward off the ill-effects of chronic stress, it can also reverse them." (Ratey, 2008e)

We need outlets for frustration, anxiety, and fear when we experience our children struggling and their future, and ours with them, is in question. Taking control of something, anything important and desirable, is an essential mechanism to provide those most necessary outlets. Physical exercise does not solve the problem that is creating the stress. It does, however, help our brain and body operate at their best. Exercising regularly gives us proof that we can take the initiative to make something in our lives change.

And even better, exercising with someone adds another protective factor to the recovery process, assisting us to turn off the stress-response at least long enough to recover. As mentioned in earlier chapters, social affiliation is a significant protective factor, producing many positive outcomes. In fact, a common practice among scientists to produce stress in rats is to remove them from their social environment. Even calves isolated for 10 weeks while weaning show less cognitive skill than those that live with a buddy. Isolation, loneliness, aloneness are not helpful states while coping with stress, and, in fact, are states that can produce stress. And the more we go without strong social affiliations, the lower our self-esteem and the higher the possibility of feeling shame about who we are and what we are dealing with in our lives.

Using exercise as an opportunity to connect with others, compounds the stress-reducing benefits that both provide. Some of us enjoy, and are very accustomed to, exercising alone. Others of us are much more likely to stay motivated for on-going exercise if we do it in a group context or with a friend or trainer. If aerobic exercise is facilitated by social connections or opportunities to build relationships, so much the better.

A 37-year-old patient, Rachael, reported having a very difficult time making friends. Although she was open to friendships and felt she initiated and demonstrated interest, friendships did not materialize. When she announced "There must be something wrong with me" and "I don't even want to look in the mirror anymore," it was clear that the original problem, which was her difficulty making friends, had now morphed into another problem. The lack of social affiliations had created lowered self-esteem and a sense of shame. Using exercise as a way to meet people can not only be an outlet for frustration, an enhancement of brain functioning, but can also be a source of self-esteem. These are all important strategies to combat the effects of prolonged stress.

As is true of most coping mechanisms, too little or too much can be harmful. Up to a point, the more you exercise, the better it is for your brain and body. Sustaining routines that support ongoing and consistent structures for exercise is more important, in my mind, than how much or hard you exercise. My 93-year-old mother announced that she was taking a Zumba® class. Having sweated through one Zumba® class myself, I was astonished that she would consider such a vigorous form of exercise. I was relieved when she added that the class was called "chair Zumba®," something I was sure she could manage.

For our purposes, we are talking about beginning to move a lot. To walk, run, spin, treadmill, dance at a reasonable level. That reasonable level needs to be determined by the state of your body and slowly challenging yourself to increase endurance, keeping in mind that the activity you choose should have some desirable aspect to it. (Don't choose swimming if you have no convenient access to a pool.) And, of course, always check with your doctor before starting an exercise program.

No one really knows how intense exercise needs to be or exactly how long it takes to promote the stress-reducing benefits. However, Benjamin Greenwood, a research associate in the Department of Integrative Physiology at the University of Colorado found that rats that ran regularly over a period of only three weeks did not demonstrate much reduction in stress-induced anxiety, compared to rats that ran over a period of six weeks. Psychologists who have studied exercise and the reduction of anxiety and depression suggest that a short, ten-minute walk can immediately improve mood. Ratey cautions that the effect of one ten-minute walk may be transitory if not reinforced on a day-to-day level. To some extent, the more stress you are experiencing, the more your body needs to move in order to provide enhanced brain functioning.

Movement is life-enhancing and it does not particularly matter what kind of movement it is. For Rebecca, my socially isolated patient who was struggling with emotionally distant adult children and depression, the choice of exercise was dance. And to *my* great surprise, she decided to take a tango class. Perfect choice. Lots of exercise, contact with males and to *her* surprise, she was quite good at it. That one choice provided her with a physical outlet for the prolonged stress she experienced dealing with her children and gave her increased social affiliation as well as a sense of empowerment that accompanies taking control of something meaningful.

Of course, none of that helped her feel less fear about her children's condition and whereabouts, but it may have given her back a life of her own, which is a difficult accomplishment when we are emotionally consumed by worry, fear, and anxiety. To survive the prolonged stress of heartbreaking parental situations, life has to encompass more than the stressors. Taking control over a meaningful area of life, for Rebecca, helped accentuate that reality.

Those of you who have exercised on a regular basis will recognize that sustained physical movement is itself a form of meditation in motion. To put energy into any form of exercise (dancing, walking, skating, running, gardening) directs attention in a purposeful way, in the present moment and possibly without self-judgment. Remember Jon Kabat-Zinns' definition of mindfulness, "...paying attention in a particular way: on purpose, in the present moment and non- judgmentally." A nice long walk with a friend, a run in the park, or even a tango class can satisfy that definition.

The more regularly we exercise, the more we wire together the activity with the positive effects. I do not particularly like to run, but I like the feeling afterwards. It has become wired in my brain that running makes me feel good. A sustained exercise routine helps wire the activity with the positive effects. We are creating a stronger and more robust connection between neurons as we keep a sustained connection between a state of mind and an activity.

Michael Hopkins, a graduate student affiliated with the Neurobiology of Learning and Memory Laboratory at Dartmouth, explains, "It looks more and more like the positive stress of exercise prepares cells to handle stress in other forms." (Reynolds, 2009) So putting stress on my muscles helps me deal with stress in my life. It is important to find ways to calm the chatter, to lessen anxiety, so we can better respond to stressors involving our children's lives and our relationships with them. Physical exercise yields multiple benefits for those dealing with on-going stressors, better equipping us to experience a life beyond the stressor.

CHAPTER 9

Who Is In Charge?

Locus of Control and Learned Helplessness

WE DISCUSSED LOCUS of control in earlier chapters, but the many facets of the subject deserve a chapter of their own. To review, locus of control is a measure of the extent to which individuals feel they can control the outcome of personal life events. In the 1950's, Julian Rotter, conceptualized an individual's locus (from the Latin word location) as either internal or external. An external locus of control reflects the belief that life is controlled by random, external events of which the individual has little or no control. An individual with a strong external locus of control views luck, chance, or fate as playing the greater role in determining the outcome of events. An internal locus of control reflects the belief that events in one's life are influenced and even controlled by reactions and responses made by the individual.

External locus of control and learned helplessness both have a connection to each other and to depression. Learned helplessness is a concept that identifies the emotional, cognitive, and behavioral outcome when an individual perceives having no control. Learned helplessness is a greater risk for those who possess an external locus of control, where life events are seen as subject to chance, luck or external forces. (Hirota, 1974)

We are most vulnerable to learning helplessness during early years of life when control over our situation is restricted. Particularly in distressed family situations, children may receive profound lessons of learned helplessness. Children from family situations that are emotionally dysregulated (overwhelmed or out of control) or abusive and who have felt helpless to alter their circumstances, are more subject to depression in later years. Depression and a sense of helplessness feed on each other. I see parents who have "tried everything" over and over again and to no avail: treatment programs, tough love, boundaries, giving up, giving in, and any other option that has presented itself. A parent who has learned the lessons of helplessness in their own childhood will be less likely to possess a high internal locus of control. If a parent is operating from a long held position of helplessness and guided by an external locus of control, taking control of significant areas of life is made more difficult.

Sadly, a patient of mine becomes teary each time I say anything positive about her. She says, "It feels so foreign and so wrong and unfamiliar." Her father had taught her to believe that she was "ugly and stupid and no one will ever want to marry you." Although she did marry and have two sons, now at 80 she continues to struggle with that long held self-view. If we go into parenting with a strong lesson of learned helplessness, taking control of what can realistically be in our control can be a more difficult maneuver.

This was demonstrated again to me when it became clear that Sharon (who offered her son her gun saying "Just shoot me ....") had lived her married life with a powerful, narcissistic husband whom her sons not only admired, but sided with against her in marital disputes. No wonder she was so without boundaries. She had learned that, no matter what she did, her husband ran the emotional show. She was afraid that she would "lose them forever" if she set strong, consistent boundaries with her sons.

To her surprise, however, taking control of a boundary regarding how she would allow herself to be treated, actually reduced her fear. An upward spiral can begin when we make a distinction between what we need to accept (for now) and what we can have impact upon. Staying aware and in charge of our own perspective, thought process, emotional regulation and behavioral responses to difficult situations provides those needed outlets to stay healthy and vital while we forge through intensely stressful experiences of heartbreak parenting. For Sharon, it is very difficult to focus on her own life, particularly in the midst of an extremely pressured family atmosphere. Her sons haven't changed, but, ever so gradually, she has. And, that's enough for now.

What we now know about learned helplessness is that it is difficult to unlearn. If we learn that outcomes are out of our control, our motivation and initiative will be lessened, and this is a state that can contribute to depression. If we have tried to influence an outcome to no avail, it is even more difficult to build hopefulness and motivation. Unsuccessful trying (and we try so hard when it comes to our children) can be an even greater blow to developing an internal locus of control than if we have not tried at all. This emphasizes the need to distinguish between what we can and cannot control. Sharon had control of how much abusive talk she would listen to, but she did not have control over her sons' negative view of her. She began directing her focus to areas of her life where she could have the greatest impact.

It is empowering when we decide to take control over areas of our lives that make us healthier, that help us feel better about ourselves and that reduce our stress. Parents of children who are struggling need that empowerment without assuming more control than they have. One of my patients made the decision to take control of eating three meals a day so she would reduce her late night binging. A healthy decision at many levels. What made the greatest impact on her, however, was how good it felt to make the decision and follow through, to be in charge. Having control over as many areas of life as possible helps move us away from a position of learned helplessness, therefore reducing the risk of depression.

Although taking control in areas of life that facilitate a desirable or positive outcome can mitigate the negative effects of learned helplessness, these changes in behavior, must be voluntary. Even rats, when freely choosing to run on a running wheel feel great (as measured by level of stress hormones,) but when forced to run on that same wheel for the same distance, their stress response increases. (Greenwood, et.al. 2003)

Here is where the difficulty comes. It may be a great decision to take control over the amount of exercise you get each day, for example. However, if you have unsuccessfully tried to make use of your gym membership, to take the dog on longer walks, or to use the treadmill that is sitting right in front of the television, then your motivation to take control of exercise will be weak because of the history of failure. That doesn't mean exercise would not be desirable, feel good, and produce favorable results, but prior experience of unsuccessful attempts will be experienced as an obstacle. We have all heard that form of learned helplessness in sayings such as, "I just can't stay with it once I start" or "It makes my muscles and joints hurt" or "Buying exercise equipment would just be a waste on me." And a new one for me to hear, "I don't like to sweat."

Actually, the last excuse is the least likely to come from a position of learned helplessness, and instead just might be an expression of lack of desire. In that case, exercise would not be a useful endeavor for building a stronger sense of control because it has no desirable outcome for her.

Taking control of things that are meaningful and desirable in some way, and which lead to positive results will steer us away from a helpless, frustrated position. Exercise will almost always lead to positive results, but not if it feels forced without desire. Going to online dating sites to meet a partner might be a very good thing to do, in terms of taking control of a meaningful area of life, but not if other's have pushed you into something you might not be ready to do. (Although a friend of mine went kicking and screaming into on-line dating, only to meet her now fiancée. So who knows.)

Seligman, in his learned helplessness experiments, observed that animals that were previously shocked with electricity no matter where they moved in their cage, later, when given the opportunity to easily move away from the shock, did not move. They became passive and did not try again. For human parents with fears and worries about struggling children, movement is needed. Moving away from a learned helplessness state of mind requires:

- Distinguishing between what to accept and what to control.
- Establishing realistic steps toward a desired goal to reduce the occurrence of "unsuccessful trying."
- Increasing behaviors that are within a parent's control and that produce positive outcomes (either for the child or for the parent)

My patient, Rita, whose daughter could not complete further college and is seemingly unmotivated to move forward and out of the house, struggled with a decision to attend a twice-a-week yoga class, followed by lunch with friends. Her concern was, "If I'm not home until afternoon, my daughter will still be asleep." Rita came to the decision that, NO, she should not even think about giving up yoga because it brought her many levels of positive returns. How long her daughter slept was not something she could control. Rita also debated whether or not to push forward with applying for disability on her daughter's behave. She wondered if that was taking control of something she should expect her daughter to do. She came to the conclusion that, YES that was something over which she should take control because it was unrealistic to expect that her daughter would take that kind of initiative. That also was something that had the potential of yielding positive outcomes, not only financially but in the form of assistance with job search. Rita needed to take control of that application process and accept that her daughter would not or could not accomplish that task.

If there is an opposite of learned helplessness, it would be empowerment. One patient of mine accuses me of using this word far too much (and you can see she is correct.) But what a wonderful, even if overused, word. Its definition refers to increasing the strength of an individual. No wonder I use it "too much." Who wouldn't want to be empowered?

The idea of empowerment as an antidote to learned helplessness was put to the test by researchers in the late 1970's with cancer and postsurgical patients. (Norman, et.al. 1978) In dealing with pain management of hospitalized patients, nursing time was consumed with requests for pain medication and with patients' intense distress in waiting for their medication. The patients had no control over the management of their pain. In this radical experiment for the time, patients whose pain medication had previously been dispensed by nurses were now given the power to self-medicate. When patients experienced too much pain, they could push a button that would dispense a measured dose of medication based on their perceived need. If they felt they needed more, they could simply push the button again.

The concern from the medical community was that patients would over-medicate, become addicted and, in general, self-medication would put too much responsibility on the patient. None of these concerns were actualized and, in fact, the amount of medication dispensed *decreased* significantly when control was put in the hands of the patient. Why should this be the case? Clearly, the sense of control and predictability (patients knowing that their medication would be available exactly when needed it) helped patients gain a sense of control over their pain, even to the point of reducing the amount of medication needed.

The question of how to reduce or eliminate learned helplessness is answered with empowerment. How to empower? Take control of as many areas of your life as you want to and are able to.

We are not necessarily talking about huge areas of life, just normal things such as:

- exercise
- social interactions
- decisions that take your needs and wants seriously in spite of the stressors
- setting boundaries
- utilizing tools such as meditation and mindfulness to reduce psychological and physiological consequences of prolonged stress

The literature tells us that taking control, in any of the ways that are possible, makes a difference. I will always remember a situation relayed to me by a young man named Devin who had grown up with a terrifyingly abusive step-father. For no apparent reason, Devin would be banished not just to his room but to a specific place on his bed and instructed by his step-father not to move a muscle until further notice. Devin told me that while sitting as still as possible, for fear his step father would come in at any time, he would pull a couple of small strings from his jacket or jeans and begin weaving them with his fingers moving only slightly. When his step-father returned he could easily hide the weaving by dropping it or putting it in the palm of his hand. This seemingly small action allowed Devin to feel a sense of control of the time in solitary confinement. The fact that he told me this story many years after the situation had occurred, revealed the importance for him of finding that control somewhere amongst a frightening and stressful life situation. The woven strings did not change anything in his step-father's abusive behavior, but they did contribute to Devin's psychological survival.

The downward spiral of depression and learned helplessness can be reduced or reversed by actions that assert control in meaningful areas of life. For Devin, he took control of the only thing he found to be within his control. And, it made a difference. That is the coping mechanism; taking control of anything that makes a positive difference in *your* life, even while life situations seem out of control.

CHAPTER 10

Outlets for Frustration

IN MANY SITUATIONS that involve fear and concern about the well-being of a child of any age, there appears to be little we can do with the overabundance of sometimes excruciatingly intense feelings. There are not many feeling states that have a greater magnitude than those regarding our children's well-being. In earlier chapters, I discussed protective factors, such as interpersonal connections, prioritizing situations that enhance your life *in spite* of the serious stressors that are on-going. I also discussed the need for physical outlets to address the buildup of stress hormones that cause damage when prolonged and consistent, and the benefit of fostering a sense of control over meaningful areas of your life.

When life circumstances flood us with intense and difficult emotions, we need outlets to filter and balance those emotions. An outlet is something that operates in your life as a distracter to the stressor. Parents who are in heartbreaking situations with their children can experience overwhelming preoccupation, emotionally and behaviorally, with the prolonged need to attend to the stressor with little or no positive result. Obviously, a child's acute needs will take priority for a parent and create an intense focus. This is as it should be. However, when prolonged, intense focus does not lead to reduction of stress, the physiological and emotional damage that we have been discussing is at risk.

All of the protective factors mentioned previously are outlets for stressful emotions. And yet, to make use of these outlets requires an almost paradigm-like shift in the way we think and feel about managing and sustaining our resources as we face heartbreak and all of its accompanying emotions. A paradigm shift is a change from one way of thinking to another. It involves a transformation, a new way of looking at things. What I consider a paradigm change in a distressed parent's thinking is this: it is essential, over time, to attend to my own live and create moments that help restore me to allostasis, no matter how intense and serious the stressor. It is essential to balance stress with relaxation and desirable preoccupations, balance fear and dread with a sense of control and acceptance, and balance isolation or aloneness with connections to, and support from, people who matter to you.

Keep in mind, this paradigm shift does not signify pulling away or being neglectful of our children's needs. It means balance, and it points to the necessity to sustain resources in order to best attend to difficult situations and emotions. I call this a paradigm shift because I have witnessed in my patients such tremendous difficulty with self-focus when their children's well-being is in question. Attending to self needs has not been on the radar.

Of course this would be true. There are situations where that paradigm shift cannot be accomplished because the terribleness of the situation just will not leave room for it. At some level, however, attention to self is imperative if we are to stay available to others, regardless of the situation. An outlet of frustration might simply be a way to look at things as they really are and a move toward acceptance. Simply having the knowledge that the effects of prolonged stress will reduce health, mental clarity, memory, and problem-solving ability may bring awareness to the task of self-care for emotionally taxed parents.

An outlet of frustration may be directed toward the other parent. Most parents know how difficult it is to be completely aligned in co-parenting a non-thriving child (or even a thriving child). The task is not to always agree or see things eye to eye, but to have developed a healthy enough relationship with your partner or spouse to be attuned to each other's vulnerabilities regarding the stressful situation.

My client, Renee, eventually moved into an apartment because she and her husband were at such odds about how they should treat their 28-year-old daughter, who was still at home and verbally abusive to them. Renee had lost respect for her husband because of his persistent denial of the problem and what she called the enabling of their daughter. He lived with the fear that his daughter would commit suicide if pressured to leave the house. Renee felt unprotected from her daughter's abusive language toward her. Her husband's relentless defense of his daughter left him blind to the effect on Renee. In turn, Renee could not offer a safe harbor for her husband's fears in that he was unable to do that very same thing for her.

Their inability to take in their spouse's fears and concerns created unresolved conflict and emotionally threatened both Renee and her husband and therefore put their relationship in jeopardy. He protected himself from his catastrophic fears by holding onto a fierce stance that his daughter should be supported to stay in the house, regardless of her behavior. Renee's protection was to leave. They did not know how to attune to each other's concerns. Being attuned to each other's feelings and fears could have enabled both of them to provide an outlet for the other and a feeling of being taken care of by their spouse. Their interactions as a couple created more stress and did not serve as an outlet for either of them. And, therefore their effectiveness with their daughter was diminished.

Recognizing the strain a non-thriving child can put on a relationship might direct a couple to get help of some kind. They each need to be an outlet for the other's emotional experience. If their own communication deficits have increased their vulnerability and sense of helplessness, they cannot (and won't want to) be an outlet for the other. Couple's therapy is one possible resource that can offer parents a chance to understand how the situation is affecting their partner and allow them to become more attuned to each other's experience. A parent with a partner has the possibility of receiving an incredible resource of support. However, the difficult situation of attending to a non-thriving child can turn that resource into a source of conflict and emotional vulnerability, serving only to escalate stress.

In many cases, outlets of frustration are hard to come by. The more we need them, the more difficult it is to prioritize them in our lives. Sharon states "I need to get away from my kids." And she desperately does. Interestingly, she planned a trip to Mexico with a friend and at the last minute (and at her most abusive son's insistence), she took her son *with* her. She is so consumed by her need to please her son that she cannot follow through with self priorities. Remember Rita who hesitated to take a yoga class because her daughter might not get out of bed if Rita was not in the house? That is just another example of how difficult it is for distressed and worried parents to prioritize their own needs and make outlets available for themselves.

No matter how old we get, it can be difficult to establish outlets for dealing with the frustrations wrapped around our children and their behavior. Mary is well into her 80's and is my oldest client. She discovered that her eldest granddaughter had been taking money from her for several years. Other family members have now confronted the situation (and all agree not to pursue criminal charges) and put a stop to it, but life goes on for the thieving granddaughter as if nothing is wrong. Mary wants answers, wants an apology, and lives with tremendous hurt, confusion, and anger. Although she does not have one-to-one contact with her granddaughter, she accepts her telephone calls only to hear her granddaughter talk about the expensive college their son will be attending and the new car they just purchased. There is never an apology or an owning of responsibility.

It would be a fair guess to say Mary's stress hormone count goes up drastically when in communication with her granddaughter.

Mary needs her granddaughter's remorse, explanation, and genuine apology in order to begin healing, and yet she hesitates to ask for it. Her fear is, "If I confront her I'll never see her again and her children will feel left out of our family." That is the same fear that drives Sharon to take her verbally abusive son to Mexico on *her* vacation.

When a fear is actualized by a child's behavior or situation, the feeling of panic caused by stress hormones flooding the system cannot be prevented. That hormone rush is to be expected and anticipated. The call from Rita's daughter's college, Claudia's son's late night call from who knows where, Laura's son's schizophrenic breakdowns all send frightening alarms to vigilant parents. There is nothing to mitigate that fearful, helpless response. What a parent *can* control are the moments in-between those stress responses. In some situations, the stress is more on-going for the parents than for the child. Parents can never let go of their fear, guilt, or worry while their children's present and future well-being is in question. These parents need those moments in-between. Stress is not necessarily harmful, but prolonged stress is. "Outlets for frustration" is just a phrase for identifying the importance of the "moments- in-between" because there is so little to do about the unpreventable hormonal response caused by our vigilant scanning for danger signals.

A patient who struggles with a drug addicted and out of control son told me of the relief she felt when she heard he was again in rehab. However, the feeling of relief sounded a different alarm for her. "I can't let myself feel relieved or hopeful because I know I will be disappointed once again." Based on her son's history, that may well be true. However, this is a moment-in-between that her brain/body so desperately needs. It is important to take a breath, to allow a moment of distraction from the stressor. Prolonged stress needs interruptions so the brain/body can find relief, even if that relief is ever so temporary.

To create those "moment in-between" we need tools to self-soothe, a subject addressed in previous chapters. Increasing both the ability to self-soothe and differentiate as well as minimizing personalization and projection are skills that help promote the emotional balance needed to create "moments in-between." Self-soothing can be made easier when we know how to breathe our way through upsetting moments. These are skills that can be strengthened by mindfulness practices. Differentiation, discussed earlier, is a way of thinking and behaving that creates a space between me and a loved one, while, at the same time, allowing connectedness and presence with that other person.

When I personalize someone else's emotion, I am very likely to respond to that someone from a defensive or disempowered position. When Sharon's sons, with great delight, tell her how useless she is because she doesn't work, she begins to tell them all about how hard she worked before she had children. She allows their words to prompt her to defend herself, giving her children more fuel for their caustic verbal engine. If she could adopt the perspective that their accusations are more about them than about her, she may be able to respond with more confidence and self-respect.

Some of the negative and hurtful expressions coming from children whose behavior breaks our hearts are not really so much about us. When we have at least a speck of a non-personalized perspective, we maximize the chance of responding effectively and reducing our own stressful reactions, thereby leaving an opening for those essential "moments in-between" the stressors. We need always to look for opportunity to recognize or create and promote those moments. Sometimes they are all we have. And sometimes they are enough to get us through.

"Moments in-between" are opportunities to restore balance to an overactive HPA loop. To create those moments, we have to maintain some awareness of what gives us pleasure, relaxation, even fun and joy. It is difficult to stay attuned to those resources when we are preoccupied, long-term, with overwhelming concerns. If you watched the television show "24," you saw a constantly and maximally stressed anti-terrorist agent who was perpetually holding hundreds of people's lives in his hands. He often had only minutes to diffuse the bomb or deter the terrorist attack or even to save his own daughter's life. When watching the show you might have wondered as I did, "When does this man ever relax, go to the bathroom, eat a meal?" The show surely won its high ratings because the intensity was stimulating, no outlets, minute-to-minute stress. Of course, as the show's title reveals, the agent only had to endure this prolonged stress for one 24-hour period. Real life under stressful conditions requires balance, allostasis, outlets and "moments-in-between" to most effectively diffuse the internal bomb and to be the best resource for our non-thriving or difficult children.

It is particularly difficult for stressed and worried parents to consider one very useful and enjoyable outlet: humor. Dr. Scott Weems, a researcher at the University of Maryland writes about the inoculating effect that humor has on stress. (Wall Street Journal, 2014) He refers to the cold pressor test which helps scientists measure pain tolerance. This test asks subjects to submerge their hands into ice water that is just above freezing. Weems states that after watching a comedy such as The Bill Cosby Show, subjects were able to achieve a higher pain tolerance than someone watching a nature documentary.

Weems refers to a study done in 2000 by Arnold Cann at the University of North Carolina. In this study, subjects watched either 16 minutes of stand-up comedy or the equivalent amount of time watching a travel show. All subjects were then asked to watch a shock film that depicted gruesome death scenes. Those volunteer subjects who first watched comedy reported significantly less "psychological distress" than did volunteer subjects who watched a travel show before the gruesome scenes. So, we might conclude that humor can be a useful tool, a distracter that serves to increase our hardiness while experiencing and reacting to stressful situations.

Humor is not only a distraction and a reminder that life is more than the stressors; it also prepares the mind, like exercise, for upcoming stressful events. To laugh together is healing and facilitates many outlets of frustration. The couple I mentioned earlier who stayed so attuned to each other during their son's cancer treatment could laugh together when the father decided to shave his head. The parents even found a way, in rare moments, to joke in frustration at the disability insurance system that presented so many obstacles to them. The group of mothers of special needs children in England, who I mentioned in an earlier chapter, could laugh as well as cry together. Both are powerful outlets.

Struggling parents often do not feel entitled to these outlets ("I crash when she crashes"). Their preoccupation with the stressful situations makes it ever so difficult to create space for themselves. A paradigm change in their thinking begins to take place as parents learn experientially that creating and utilizing outlets in their lives are prerequisites to health and resourcefulness. Of course the paradox is always that by making space for themselves, they fortify their ability to be present with clarity and receptiveness to the ongoing needs of their children's situations and behaviors.

CHAPTER 11

Exhausted With Parenting

"I'M EXHAUSTED WITH parenting," Roberta said as she sank wearily into my office couch. Both of her adult sons were still living at home, one seemingly motivated to get a job and live independently and the other less motivated to create an exit plan. Both of her children have experienced depression to the point of openly considering suicide, creating a soup of emotions for Roberta as she attempts to move them forward and outward. I assured her there was nothing abnormal about her "exhaustion" when it comes to parenting, and it was not a reflection of how much she loved her children.

What this does bring to light is the reality that for most parents, there is something like a shelf life on stage-dependent parenting. By stage-dependent, I am talking about how our tasks as parents morph into different requirements as we follow the stages of our children's development. When my youngest daughter was about nine or ten, I accepted a 'play date' on her behalf. Well, I had forgotten to check in with her development and, somewhere along the line, that had become unnecessary and definitely unwanted behavior on my part. She would decide who she wanted to play with and, yes, I could do the arranging, but not the decision making. I could drop that task from my parental duties.

A friend of mine, who was very close to his daughter, was hurt and shocked when his daughter, for the first time, ignored him completely at a middle school function and turned toward her friends as if he did not exist. Well, it was *that* stage of development for his daughter and his role was changing quite appropriately. He just needed to advance along with her development. It hurt his feelings, but would he really want anything different? No, we want our children to keep moving, keep maturing, keep developing toward independence. Our roles change as our children develop and that is exactly what we want. Ideally, we will parent our children in ways that match the stage of development that they are experiencing. I read somewhere that if parents let go of about 10% of control every year after age six, we will be in just about the right place by the time our children are preparing to leave home. That would be responding to the reality that our children are changing and developing and our roles need to change with that developmental process.

Misappraisals of the stages of development, like my underestimation of my daughter's social decision making, can happen in the opposite direction as well. A patient of mine treats her 10-year-old daughter as if she is in a more advanced stage of development than her years, partly because her daughter is intellectually gifted and emotionally insightful. My patient confides in her daughter like she would confide in a friend. She discusses problems that should be left to adults to resolve and shares activities with her that would be much more enjoyable for an adult. At age ten, her daughter is still a child, and the parenting tasks need to correspond to that stage. Her daughter is not yet ready to be her mother's confidant.

When my eldest daughter was three years old, I remember saying to friends, "If she could just stay this sweet forever." My brother-in-law was known to say about his gorgeous daughter, "I don't want her to date until she's 30." Obviously these statements are about the wish that our children could stay in a certain stage of development. But of course that isn't what we really want. What if they didn't move forward? What if they didn't continue to move into emerging stages of development? Then we would become exhausted.

A couple I am seeing has a new baby who is now six months old. They are already exhausted with the predictable sleepless nights, feeding complications, and lack of time for themselves. But now the baby is advancing in her development. She smiles and plays with them, and greets them with elation after a short separation. They are no longer exhausted in the same way because new development brings new tasks, new challenges, and new joys (and different reasons to be exhausted).

How long would we be content with the role of diaper changer or chauffer or homework helper or with the stress of college applications? Parents become exhausted if stages of development do not move forward. We may be fearful of our child beginning to drive, but what if she didn't? We may agonize over the thought of our child leaving for college, but what if he didn't?

That is what parents experience with children who don't or can't keep moving through healthy stages of development. Kids who get stuck in the process of moving forward, or whose relationships with parents become adversarial, oppositional, or even abusive, will exhaust almost any parent. It is important to understand this experience of exhaustion as something to be expected and yet something that needs attention. An exhausted parent needs to take care of him/herself and be free of self-judgment. Exhaustion is not the same as giving up.

We attend to physical exhaustion by resting, taking time off, distracting ourselves with a vacation, or providing self-care in some manner. Emotional exhaustion, due to a lack of movement through the stages of development or to tiresome interactions with our children, must also be given the same non-judgmental attention. Acknowledging the physical and mental demands of this parenting role, attending to yourself in a way that brings back energy, continuing to look for areas of life which can be under your control, and utilizing outlets for frustration are necessary supports to facilitate clear thinking. These tools facilitate the ability to be present and reflective in the difficult situations of parenting children who have not progressed in their development or have moved along in ways that create pain and frustration, fear and concern.

The experience of exhaustion simply tells the parent, "I need to replenish my energy." As parents get caught up in the struggles of, or with, their children, paying attention to their own physical and mental states can get overlooked. It is important to be vigilant about exhaustion, without judgment, because, unattended to, it can increase the risk of depression and activation of the whole HPA loop that I discussed earlier. It helps to have developed a "replenishing manual" of your own. The manual would answer the question, "What can I do when I have become exhausted with my role as a parent in this particular situation with my child?" Do I seek out friends, exercise more, or use my spouse or partner to help improve my mood? Do I go to a spa or just get space away for even a small amount of time? Do I use mindfulness practices to help soothe and calm my HPA loop? Whatever your strategies, it is helpful to have practiced using them so they are accessible to you during the times when you have the least energy to create them.

I see it like practicing CPR on the manikin or practicing disaster procedures over and over so those skills stay sharp and can be put into place when needed. You can expect to become exhausted. If you have developed ways to respond to that understandable emotional and physical fatigue by identifying what best uplifts you, what distracts you in a positive way, what activities are stress-reducing, and who are the 'go to' people in your life who offer comfort and understanding, then you won't get stuck in exhaustion. Instead you will be better prepared to embrace the ebb and flow, to respond with acceptance and lack of judgment. And, we must always be watchful for negative self-judgment. Who would *not* be exhausted with an ever-present and prolonged stressful environment?

Reducing judgment seems to be a particularly difficult issue. When my patient said, "I'm exhausted with parenting," she then added, "Is that a bad thing to say?" Exhaustion will often come when there is a lack of movement or when movement is in the wrong direction. We get exhausted dealing with the same issues over and over again. We become exhausted emotionally when we feel stuck in the same place. We become exhausted when our actions seem to yield no positive resolution. No, it is not a bad thing to say. It is an understandable reality and needs to be responded to with acceptance rather than self-judgment and a replenishing plan.

CHAPTER 12

Canary in the Coal Mine

CANARIES ARE KNOWN to be quite sensitive to methane and carbon monoxide, the very gases that build up in a coal mine when the mine is not equipped with a well functioning ventilating system. When these gases are present, the canary will die. This alerts the miner who carries the bird on his shoulder to get out quickly and bring his friends with him. Unfortunately for the canary, it acts as a valuable alarm to which the miner will pay close attention. I have used this example as a metaphor in couple's therapy, encouraging one partner to be the canary for the other. Let your partner know when he or she is doing something dangerous to the relationship. And of course, the partner must be open to listen to the alarm.

Body awareness can be a valuable canary in our own lives. Signals from our body are often missed or overlooked. Lack of attention to this implicitly truthful and constantly available source of feedback diminishes our capacity for control and awareness, which is badly needed when confronting over-the-top stresses in our already stressful lives. The worry and intense emotions that entangle us when responding to our children's struggles, or to our struggles with our children, create over-the-top stresses. We need the canary. Body awareness is a rich source of information regarding how we are physiologically processing stress, and as such, is a barometer of well-being or danger.

When Barbara (who struggles with an unmotivated and depressed adult daughter living at home) received the results of her blood tests that indicated imminent danger, she began to redirect at least a portion of her focus to her physical self-care. The canary had not died yet, but it was on its last leg. Given there was heart disease in her family, Barbara now took the grim test results seriously. Many other danger signals had pre-dated the lab results but had been overlooked and dismissed because there had been "too many other things to worry about." Physical symptoms such as trouble with sleep, fatigue, weight problems, chest pains, and lack of endurance had all been evident but were ignored. She had not attended to her diet and exercised infrequently. Barbara's canary was screaming but nobody had been listening.

I was intrigued by the shallow breathing of another patient who suffered from anxiety. I had never observed anyone who could breathe so shallowly and still be alive. Her breath seemed to go no further than her upper throat, which perhaps accounted for her hoarse voice. I brought attention to her breathing pattern and began some breathing exercises with her. As she began to breathe more deeply, bringing her breath closer and closer to her diaphragm, tears came pouring out. She had been afraid to breathe, afraid to face the reality of her very unhappy life with an emotionally abusive husband. Allowing herself to experience that fear and sadness did not change anything about her life circumstances. It did, however, help her see her life more clearly.

Clarity, even though it may not change the external situation, is a valuable state to achieve in that it promotes problem solving and decision making. My patient who had shallow breathing was silencing herself out of fear. Developing an assertive voice might provide her a sense of control of certain aspects of her life. To repeat, the more control we can take in our own lives, the less helpless we feel. And the less helplessness we experience, the less we are at risk of becoming stuck and immobile.

Attention to the nuances of our body rhythm (restriction, pain, softness, relaxed or tense muscles, shallow or deep breathing) gives us a yardstick, an awareness, a canary to direct us out of the mine. We can learn to deepen our breath. We can learn to relax our muscles. We can move in-spite of emotional pain. Our bodies can inform us of how well we are taking care of ourselves. Through body awareness, we can recognize held-in feelings that would serve us better if they were out in the open.

In some circumstances, even the thought of attending to ourselves when our children are floundering does not come up on the radar. We may be just too consumed with distressing emotion to know how to create space for that kind of self-attention. The ability to pay attention to the stress signals that develop in our bodies can be fine tuned through practice and awareness.

How do we stay alert to the canary's chirpings? Of course the first step is to acknowledge the body's messages of danger. We do this by paying attention to self-care rituals or the lack of them, to the condition of our bodies, to the effects of stress on our well-being. Bodily symptoms that should sound the alarm include:

- High blood pressure
- gastrointestinal symptoms
- sleeplessness
- rock-like shoulder muscles
- pain
- loss of energy
- listlessness
- flat emotions
- joylessness
- overall body tension

Body awareness does not come naturally to most people. I use the Jacobson relaxation exercise to make that awareness easier. This exercise simply involves tensing and releasing different muscle groups individually. You start with your feet, curling them up as tightly as you can (without cramping) and then slowly releasing the muscles. I have patients do that foot exercise several times before moving up to the leg muscles and continuing, one muscle group at a time, all the way up to the neck and face muscles. Tensing the muscles brings awareness to that muscle group and makes it easier to let go of tension.

Remember Todd who experienced himself caught between his wife and son? Todd knew his stress level was escalating when his son inappropriately spent college money and threatened to drop out of school without further financial assistance. He did not want his son to drop out of school. That would create even more stress for Todd. However, he recognized the manipulation on his son's part and knew that he would be enabling him by providing more money.

Todd had a history of past health problems and he recognized the need to rely on rituals such as daily exercise when stress escalated. He also knew that he should not turn down traveling assignments from work (which he had done in previous crises) because of the increased stress his son's behavior was creating. Regardless of the decision he and his wife make about how best to respond to their son, Todd recognized that he needed to turn his attention to himself. He heard the canary. In previous years, Todd would have had no energy left for himself. Despair and a sense of hopelessness would have enveloped him and his work performance would have suffered. His worry about his son had been all-encompassing.

Todd anticipated what his body needed and took actions that helped mitigate the HPA loop and lessen the chance of allostatic load. He came to know his body. He continued with activities that distracted him from the stressors, and attended to physical exercise. He learned how to respond to the stress without being consumed by it. If we can recognize the danger signals, there are many areas of our lives that we can put more in our control. Body awareness is an assessment tool, a barometer to help promote allostasis, the balancing act of stress management. Attention to our bodies gives us the wherewithal to respond to the canary's message.

There is a sense of aliveness that comes from intentional focus. Of course, that is the idea behind mindfulness and other meditation practices discussed in earlier chapters. Attending to the stress we experience in our bodies opens us to the possibility of attending also to the joyful experiences in life. "Joy arises when we are open to both the beauty and the suffering inherent in living." (Brach, 2013b) I realize that this is a difficult concept for parents who are engulfed in worry, and even terror, about the outcome of their children's life situations. Joy? This requires another paradigm change.

Body awareness opens our senses; it does not dismiss or push away the suffering. Grasping onto negative feelings, as if they are a life preserver hurled out to a troubled swimmer in a turbulent sea, is sometimes the only option a parent under stress can see. A college boyfriend of mine, who was a lifeguard at a community pool, once described to me how difficult it was to rescue someone panicking and on the verge of drowning. This was not because it was difficult to retrieve the person, but because the desperate swimmer's need to grasp on was so fierce. The struggling swimmer might grasp desperately onto the lifeguard's head or shoulders, pushing him down into the water and making it difficult for both of them to breathe. The swimmer is too desperate to let go, to pause and allow himself to be rescued. In situations of heartbreak parenting, the true life preserver is to let go long enough to assess the damage and begin repair, to let yourself be rescued by your own increased self-attention and body awareness.

Remember Teresa saying, "I wake up each morning with terror"? There is no possibility that she would wake up with joy, given that her daughter has an alcohol addiction and is somewhere out there perhaps sleeping in the woods. And that is not the point. However, creating moments when your body is relaxed, and when you are able to take in small pleasures and moments of contentment, that *is* the point.

Tara Brach, a renowned meditation teacher and lecturer states, "Have the intention to hold gently the difficulties." Even when our children's circumstances are deeply disturbing to us, it is essential to practice being aware and focusing on the full scope of emotional experiences. "Be fully aware of your body, of sensation and aliveness. We're not a culture of savoring. ...we don't pause. We don't spend much time with our senses awake." (Brach 2013a) I have discussed the importance of that pause she is referring to, creating a space between you and the stress, a small moment to differentiate you from the stressors. And perhaps in those brief moments, there could be joy.

CHAPTER 13

Window of Tolerance

The Bigger the Better

A WINDOW OF tolerance is the mental area or zone of emotional arousal in which an individual can regulate intense feelings without being consumed by them. Siegel describes the window as "a band of arousal within which an individual can function well." (Siegel, 2010h) We want the "band" to be as wide as possible.

Remember Rita deciding to take her yoga class in the mornings even though she was concerned that her daughter Jennifer, without Rita there to wake her up, would still be in bed by the time she returned home? Rita learned, by considering her own needs even while concerned about her daughter, that she could comfortably manage her concern about her daughter's wasted day without interfering with her yoga class. She was learning to widen her window of tolerance, to manage her fear and frustration, which provided space to attend to her own life. She could attend her class without constant preoccupation with the situation that would quite likely be waiting for her when she returned home. And, when she got home, she possibly could deal even better with the situation after attending a yoga class.

When extremely stressful experiences push us out of our window of tolerance, our reactions will become survival oriented. Much of how we learn to survive outside that window is learned early in life. If our early models for handling stress have taught us to be reactive, defensive, leaning toward fight or flight reactions, then our thinking will likely be less clear, and we will be vulnerable to feeling emotionally flooded and overwhelmed. A patient of mine becomes what his wife calls "a deer in the headlights" and highly defensive whenever confronted with her negative reactions to him. He learned to survive his childhood by fight or flight. And with his wife, he does a bit of both. He has low tolerance for uncomfortable interpersonal situations; for anything that he would consider critical or attacking. Their relationship suffers because of his narrow window of tolerance. Too much time in their relationship is spent with either her holding in feelings because of past experiences of unsuccessful interactions with him or with him reacting defensively. He, and they, would benefit if he could build a wider window of tolerance for interpersonal conflict which would give him an opportunity to respond non-defensively and with greater mental clarity and less reactivity.

Or, our early models may have taught us, when dealing with overwhelming stress, to withdraw into states of helplessness, hopelessness and perhaps depression. This withdrawal makes life quite restricted. Laura, whose mentally ill son will not stop drinking, responded to emotionally painful interactions with her son by withdrawing from social contacts and physical activity. She stayed alone in her house, sometimes not even answering the phone. Her window of tolerance was narrow and restrictive.

There are, of course, many windows of tolerance in our lives. One person's window may be quite broad for a certain kind of stress but quite narrow for another. The traumas and negative circumstances involving our children push heavily at the outer limits of our tolerance. This stressful material challenges our ability to be calm, receptive, and present. These are emotional states that are important to achieve since they can increase effectiveness in problem solving and ward off the damage that comes with prolonged stress. Widening the window of tolerance allows an individual to stay present with and process even the extremely difficult emotions regarding heartbreak parenting.

One of my daughters recently asked me how she could over-come her fear of job interviewing. Knowing that she had a job interview the next day, it was clear she was looking for a technique or answer that could be quickly utilized. She was actually asking, "How can I widen my window of tolerance for performance anxiety and fear of rejection."

Widening a window of tolerance involves strengthening the ability to stay present with uncomfortable feelings, in this case anxiety, without judgment, while utilizing self-soothing mechanisms such as breathing and muscle relaxation practices. The window builds as we successfully self-soothe our way through difficult situations and emotions. The window builds as we experience ourselves as calmer, clearer, and more effective in these difficult situations.

My client who became a "deer in the headlights" had to alter his internal assessment regarding his wife's angry or disappointed feelings. Instead of framing his partner's negative feelings as an attack on him, he began to at least consider the possibility that her honesty with him was an expression of her great desire to make their relationship work.

To widen our window of tolerance we need to bring all resources on board:

- Interpersonal support (affiliation with those who under-stand, care, and will make themselves available)
- Physical outlets to accommodate, during stress, the body's preparation for action (exercise or movement of some sort)
- Self-soothing tools (mindfulness, breathing and relaxation practices, positive self-talk)
- Taking charge of meaningful areas of life (and acceptance of what you can't control)
- Incorporating a non-judgmental stance toward self and others; viewing self-blame as ineffective and non-productive. (That doesn't mean ignoring responsibility when appropriate.)

Widening the window of tolerance involves accepting that the stressors and the struggles may not change, but the ability to stay present with calm and clear thinking and to operate within a broad window of tolerance can expand. The more we experience ourselves in a broad window of tolerance, the easier it becomes to stay there. The more we effectively use the above mentioned tools, the more effective we become at using those tools. Just like exercising a muscle, we build capacity by practice and reinforcement.

As I mentioned in the Canary in the Coal Mine chapter, if you pay attention to your body, it will inform you when you are operating outside a window of tolerance. Of course, we all operate outside a window of tolerance part of the time, and for some of us maybe most of the time. The goal is to increase the times we can respond to upsetting, frustrating, and stressful situations involving our children while operating within a window of tolerance. We can broaden the window of tolerance by first recognizing when we are outside of it. Those are the times when the HPA loop is firing in such a way to send stress hormones to the body, activating the whole physiological stress loop. These are times when we are in the greatest agony and the least effective in problem solving.

As described previously, my patient Barbara had been living outside her window of tolerance. She had not paid attention to how much damage she was doing to her body until blood tests sounded the alarm. A seemingly slight adjustment in her perspective was actually a significant broadening of her window of tolerance. If you recall, Barbara began to focus on things important to her by starting a non-profit business and attending to her weight gain. She, of course, continued to respond to the issues that arose from her daughter Lindsay's lack of motivation and isolation but her fear was somewhat reduced and her resolve to maintain boundaries became a self mandate.

Gaining badly needed emotional support from her husband was difficult to accomplish. However, he could provide physical support to allow her more flexibility with her time. She made good use of this resource, taking control of what she could and accepting what she was most likely not going to be able to change. For Barbara, gaining support where she could and accepting what was not in her control helped her operate from a wider window of tolerance more of the time.

When we talk about windows of tolerance, we are talking about the regulation of emotions, and that has been the focus of most of this book. Emotional regulation involves using all the resources mentioned in prior chapters to prevent or reduce allostatic load. One source of regulation can be achieved through our primary relationships. Interactive regulation involves soothing intense emotions through attunement (being on the same page) with another person. It involves another person knowing you well, non-judgmentally, and understanding your reactions.

Attunement creates a sense of safety and security which can offer support for widening windows of tolerance in troubling times. To be truly known by another person is powerfully intimate and provides validation of our emotional experiences. The safety, security and validation that is provided when another person is non-judgmentally attuned to you, is a self-soothing tool that can help widen windows of tolerance for emotionally difficult situations. As my "deer in the headlights" patient began to feel safer with his partner and experienced her as understanding his reactions rather than judging them, he was able to tolerate more and more of her honest revealing of difficult feelings. And, once again, the positive spiral takes effect; the more he could tolerate her negative feelings, the more loving and hopeful she became. The more loving and hopeful she became, the easier for him to stay present and widen his window of tolerance for interpersonal feedback.

Even with stressors as intense and critical as the welfare of our children, we can expand the time we spend in a mentally safe, secure, and regulated state. The more we develop that capacity, the more capable we become to stay present through our children's struggles and difficult behavior. We can better attend to other's emotions when we can regulate our own. By now, of course, you recognize that this is the major theme of this book. We are more effective in dealing with distressing situations involving our children when we know how to support our own emotional stability and stamina.

CHAPTER 14

Reframing

"If you are distressed by anything external, the pain is not due to the thing itself but to your own estimate of it; and this you have the power to revoke at any moment."

— MARCUS AURELIUS

WELL, THAT'S A hard quote to swallow if you perceive your children in harm's way, emotionally or physically. There is not always a solution or an answer that will mitigate the circumstances that create, for parents, such deeply felt concern regarding their children. Of course, in many of the heartbreaking circumstances that parents face, change can come about through intervention or naturally occurring maturation and development.

In some tragic situations, the heartbreak worsens. And, as I stated in the preface, this is a book about the well-being of parents in a multitude of all-encompassing emotional situations. The pain may not change, but our attitude toward it can. "To a great extent, our ability to influence our circumstances depends on how we see things." (Kabat-Zinn, 1990a) How we see things can be influenced by the degree of control we experience in our lives and our ability to reflect clearly on our circumstances. How we view our life stressors can alter the outcome of the situation, for the parent or the child, or perhaps for both. Sapolsky puts it this way. "Change even the way a rat perceives its world, and you dramatically alter the likelihood of its getting a disease." (Sapolsky, 1994)

Parents who face deeply stressful situations often find themselves either in the center of a storm or emotionally and physically preparing for a storm. Reframing refers to the ability to stand at least slightly out of the center of the storm, creating enough space to choose where and how to focus attention. This is the receptive stance that promotes the ability, not to solve the problem, but to see it through the clearest lens possible. Tools that promote clarity discussed in earlier chapters include:

Differentiation

- Creating a space to live outside the realities of our children
- Increasing our ability to attune to another person while maintaining self-awareness

Managing the danger of prolonged stress

- Becoming aware of the damaging effects of stress in the body
- Utilizing self-soothing techniques such as breathing exercises and body scanning

Choosing where to focus attention

- Understanding that you do indeed have a choice, if only for moments of time
- Choosing and valuing self-care strategies that facilitate the ability to attend to others

Acknowledging difficult feelings without being consumed by them

- Staying slightly out of the center of the storm

- Adopting the belief that there is more to life than just the difficult feelings

Gaining control of meaningful areas of life

- Identifying where you can take more control of life situations
- Increasing areas of control to reduce helplessness and risk of depression

Acceptance and Receptivity

- Working *with* emotional pain that may never go away
- Realizing that acceptance does not mean giving up and instead can open possibilities

Allowing joy in spite of the painful situation

- Paying attention to and savoring small pleasures
- Allowing pleasure to exist without guilt in the presence of pain

Reframing involves attitude, belief system and perception. I am referring to a mind-set, a way of thinking about emotionally difficult experiences that are on-going and push on our most acute vulnerability: the well-being of our children. Reframing involves recognition that we cannot escape emotionally difficult experiences. It may seem that others suffer less, and that may be true. However, no one escapes the reality that life is laced with negative emotions such as grief, sadness, fear, anxiety, and guilt. When our children are at the root of that emotional difficulty, we can only work toward staying fully present in their life situations. We will enhance our ability to stay present by allowing space to also attend to our own mind and body. That is the paradigm-like change in mind-set to which I have been referring.

Perception plays a significant role in directing our emotional response and, consequently, our behavioral response to external situations. Perception is the way we think about or understand someone or something. Our perception of a situation greatly influences our appraisal of that situation (is it bad or good, a threat or not, within my window of tolerance or not) and, of course, our behavior and emotional reactions are influenced by that appraisal. Our perceptions of a situation or event are influenced by the assessment we make regarding the strength of our coping skills, available resources, degree of social support, individual personality, life experiences and locus of control.

An example is Laura, whose schizophrenic son refused medication or treatment and continued drinking while requesting money and other supports from her. She appraised her situation as, "I can't deal with him. I can't talk about it to anyone. Somehow I have failed him. I was too busy with my own difficulties when he was growing up." That appraisal leads to enormous guilt, shame and a sense of helplessness and hopelessness. She is alone, has few social supports and has not developed, throughout her life, healthy coping skills. Her behavioral response is governed by this appraisal, thus she isolates herself, using eating as a coping mechanism, and has difficulty being productive or soliciting resources.

How we assess our resources and capacity to deal with an emotionally difficult situation directs how we feel and how we react to that situation. Not so different than the assessment we might make of a physical challenge. Can I handle that hike up that mountain? Can I take that job that would require me to lift fifty pounds? Our assessment of our own resources and coping skills will influence how we perceive a situation. The more our experiences inform us that we have capacity, effective coping skills, a supply of resources and support, the more likely we will be to respond to stressful situations without resorting to unhealthy behavior or conclusions about ourselves that only serve to exacerbate emotional pain.

If I build my endurance, strengthen my muscles, I may be able to say yes to the hike and yes to the job requirement. Building resources and strengthening coping skills can alter my perception and increase my window of tolerance. The emotional pain may not change, but the attitude and response to it can. That change in attitude is facilitated by a mind-set that can encompass the view that life needs to be more than the stressors and the dictate to watch, with vigilance, for possibilities that things may be getting better (even if ever so subtly.) "You are more than this hurt. Remember who you really are." Kornfield, 2011.

An older patient of mine, Maxine, had precious, sentimental jewelry stolen from her and sold for drugs by her youngest granddaughter who had been living with her. The hurt and rage Maxine experienced seemed to have no outlet. Her granddaughter moved out of the house but only to encounter dubious living situations. Now Maxine not only experienced rage and hurt from her granddaughter's behavior but also fear for her granddaughter's safety. It can be tough holding onto such contradictory feelings. A term for that is cognitive dissonance, holding two or more incompatible feelings or thoughts at the same time. If I am offered an interview in New York for a very desirable job and yet I live in Seattle and I am afraid to fly, something will have to give. Either I convince myself that the job really wouldn't be good for me, thus reducing the dissonance, or I find a way to combat my fear of flying (by using drugs or flying with a friend) which would also reduce the dissonance.

Maxine had to give up enough of the rage and hurt to reach out to her granddaughter and offer assistance. Maxine kept a strong boundary, however, by not allowing her granddaughter to move back into her home (and she now kept her valuables under lock and key.) The painful feelings of betrayal did not go away, nor did her mistrust of her granddaughter. However, she moved to a place of accepting that, while she could not trust this young woman, she also could not live with fears for her granddaughter's safety. Although the hurt and lack of trust did not go away, her anger reduced as she took herself out of cognitive dissonance by seeing clear choices and taking control of those choices. It was no longer, as she had said initially, her granddaughter "backing me up against a wall." It was now a choice Maxine made with a clear lens. She was able to change her perspective of the situation. The way Maxine chose to deal with her situation, and the difficult feelings that surrounded the circumstances, allowed her to gain clarity in the face of incompatible feelings.

Todd is another example of gaining a perspective that promoted clarity in the face of incompatible feelings. He wanted his son to stay in college, fearing the path he would travel if he dropped out (and perhaps moved home!) At the same time, he did not want to reinforce the manipulation and the bad position his son's behavior forced upon him. His son had inappropriately spent college money without concern and had performed badly academically. He now expected Todd to cover that financial indiscretion and continue to support him in college.

Todd came to realize that *he* had to choose what course of action fit best for him and his wife. He did not want his son to drop out, so he worked out a contract that would allow his son to take a loan that had conditions and strict oversight. The stress reducer was Todd's ability to take control of developing and implementing a strategy, even though all the risk for his son's college success still remained. Regardless of what the outcome may be, he felt in control of his decision instead of perceiving the situation as a "no choice" dilemma. He had to move toward accepting that there might be nothing he could do to influence the outcome (his son's academic success), but he had looked at the situation with a clear reflection of his son's needs as well as the needs of his family. He was not "backed into a corner with no good choice."

In the situations we are addressing, focusing on self-needs is not at the expensive of the needs of others. When it comes to our children, this is often the erroneous perception. Increasing awareness of self through focus on body, attitude, resources, needs, control, acceptance, etc. can facilitate our ability to be present and available to the demands of stressful interpersonal situations. If that focus helps us to set clear boundaries, develop effective strategies, promote acceptance and control, or increase clarity, then the harmful, non-facilitative effects of stress can be reduced. And that will be good for everyone.

CHAPTER 15

"I Can Only Be as Happy as My Most Unhappy Child"

Myths and Misconceptions

A PATIENT SAID in passing, "You've probably heard the saying 'You can only be as happy as your most unhappy child.'" Well no, I had not heard it, and in fact, I found it to be a most disturbing statement, even though I realized how true it feels to parents. It implies a lock-down on a parent's ability to create happiness, and it speaks of a co-dependency that may well feel accurate to a struggling parent but offers a very limiting perspective regarding tumultuous and heartbreaking parent/child relationships.

When things are not going as we think they should, when our relationships with our children are punctuated with struggle, we are more vulnerable to developing a belief system to explain why such a thing is happening to us when it appears not to be happening to others. I recently had a patient tell me that she felt there was a curse on her. She and her husband had adopted two children from birth and both of these children had severe and unanticipated learning disabilities that only became evident as their development progressed. My patient and her husband had wanted three children, but she dared not tempt fate (or the curse) by adopting a third. This is a bright, accomplished woman not prone to irrational thinking. The idea of there being a curse on her regarding children was not only limiting but also contributed to feelings of shame and anger.

Early childhood experiences, in our families of origin, have great influence on psychosocial and emotional development. These early experiences also impact our ability to have securely attached relationships in adult life. Because of that reality, it is easy to feel guilty if we see problems in our children's development. Maxine, whose granddaughter stole jewelry from her to buy drugs, wondered with dismay if she and her deceased husband had made a mistake in raising their granddaughter. Had they been too old to take on that responsibility? Did they cater to her needs too much? Did they give her too much attention, too much of everything she asked for, too much doting, too much freedom? Her granddaughter's behavior spoke loudly toward a diagnosis of a personality disorder, something not easily attributed to parenting style. As far as I could determine, her granddaughter had been given a loving and respectful family environment. Surely they had make mistakes, as is true in all families, but the ingredients of a healthy upbringing seemed to have been in place.

The self-blame Maxine experienced served to ignite the grief she felt for the loss of her husband two years prior to the incident. She believed that her husband would have been devastated if he had been aware that his adored granddaughter was capable of such a dishonest and thoughtless act. Maxine also knew that she desperately needed his help to endure her granddaughter's indiscretion but must instead deal with it without him.

Maxine's self-blame and guilt subsided as she came to understand that her granddaughter's behavior was not necessarily explained by the parenting she and her husband had provided. The disruption to the family dynamic is just as difficult, but Maxine now can focus on what she needs to do to move forward by setting boundaries that accommodate her own needs rather than being consumed by guilt and regret. Those boundaries lie somewhere between protecting herself from further hurt and keeping the door open to the possibility of repair of the relationship with her granddaughter. What others think she should do is not as important to her as identifying what she needs and wants, and that turns out to be important in her own development.

Another commonly seen misconception involves couples who grapple with child/stepchild issues in such a way that divides them and puts them at odds with each other, rather than strengthening the couple bond and promoting mutual problem solving and emotional support. If the child divides the couple, a powerful resource for that child is diminished. In an earlier chapter I discussed Renee, whose husband continued to provide for his adult daughter's demands in the face of Renee's disagreement with his acquiescence. Ultimately she felt such a strong sense of her husband's dismissal of her feelings, providing her no protection from her daughter's verbal abuse, that she left the house permanently.

Renee's husband's belief was that their daughter's needs came first. This was a distorted perspective of their situation. He was afraid, understandably, of his daughter's suicidal thinking and therefore reluctant to support his wife's appraisal of the situation. That is a distorted view because the best thing for the daughter would be for her parents to be united in their approach to her, coming together with their differences. Gaining mutual attunement to each other's feelings, problem solving together, holding each other's needs at least as important as their daughter's needs, could strengthen their united front and could have promoted closeness within the couple.

Renee was not bound by the "I can only be as happy as my most unhappy child" mantra. Her husband, however, was. He could not see anything more important than attending to his daughter, not even his wife's sense of abandonment. He was not attuned to his wife's feelings and that oversight cost him his relationship with her. Furthermore, his situation with his daughter, and his daughter's development, have not changed, "I can only be as happy as my most unhappy child" will keep him bound to what he perceives to be his daughter's needs. Now he must also deal with the loneliness and insecurity he experiences without his wife. No gain for anyone.

When a couple is skilled in dealing with their disagreement with each other, the mutual support and clarity that arises from this vantage point offers the adult child a consistent message, and perhaps a push in a healthy direction. Emotional support within the couple serves to tighten an intimate connection and strengthens their ability to be a resource for their child. Their own happiness will be affected by, but not bound to, the degree of happiness their child is experiencing at this particular point in time. Being affected by a child's unhappiness or lack of movement cannot be avoided. However, a parent's needs must be acknowledged if that parent is to remain a stable resource for the child.

The younger the child, the more we are aware of the priority of their needs. A couple's ability to stay connected to each other's needs does not decrease their responsiveness to their children's need, regardless of the age of the child. When a couple can use effective communication to support each other in the face of parenting decisions and emotional reactions, they can then remain a united front: the state that is most conducive to parental effectiveness.

When a child is at an age when parents have to decide how to handle difficult situations such as drug use, verbal abuse, social isolation, or an adult child stuck in the basement, the couple's need for communication skills that promote attunement, connection and mutual empathy becomes heightened. With healthy, loving parents, taking the perspective that the couple always comes first will not be confused with neglect of the child. Children of all ages need healthy parents who know how to attune to each other as well as to them. Those relationship skills provide an essential model for our children in their own adult relationships.

Another myth I have encountered is that somehow the job here is to make sense of the situation, to make sense of the unfairness.

There is no making sense of pain and suffering except if we view them as part of life, unwelcomed but inevitable, having no other meaning and no other purpose. Even though the heartbreak of our children's situations can provide an opportunity for much self-learning, the search for a greater meaning or purpose, although perhaps found religiously or philosophically, can for the most part lead to erroneous and stressful conclusions.

The woman I spoke of earlier who had adopted two children from birth, both of whom have rather severe learning disabilities, concluded that "the universe is trying to tell me something." That conclusion put her in conflict with her husband with whom she had shared the desire to have three children. She had not changed her desire to have another child, but it was difficult for her to move past what she considered to be a curse.

"We can only be as happy as our most unhappy child." I understand the origin of that phrase, as does every loving parent. However, when our children's situations or behaviors are creating intense heartbreak, we cannot afford to lock into that dictate of unhappiness. If our children are unhappy or creating unhappiness, our experiences with them will, of course, be different than if they were thriving in the world and in their relationships with us.

The job I see for parents in these situations is to build internal and external resources, to differentiate, even to the smallest degree, so that life is NOT bound to the level of unhappiness of their children. Parents who can find a path that reduces dangerous stress levels and facilitates healthy life and relationship experiences, *in spite of the heartbreak*, offer a greater resource to their children and greater clarity in problem-solving and decision making for themselves. Therefore, I would change the phrase to, "I can only be as happy as I allow myself to be." Much more to the point when surviving heartbreak parenting.

CHAPTER 16

Reflections

WHEN STRESS CANNOT be turned off because we are consumed by the emotional intensity of a stressor, we create a dangerous loop, an unhealthy environment for our mind and body. In addition, we decrease our likelihood of approaching problems with mental clarity and calmness, thus rendering ourselves less effective in responding to problematic situations. Life in modern times will never lack stressors. Our bodies are well equipped to respond. However, the emotional intensity of heartbreak kids creates special stressors that can consume parents and bog down life.

The greatest resource for a parent dealing with difficult issues with their children is their own ability to differentiate (or create a space) between themselves and their children. In this space lies the possibility of a non-reactive, fully present, mentally clear, and emotionally calm resource for the child. That space also allows for a life *for* the parent, an opportunity to build resources and attend to self-care. When our children are not thriving in the important areas of their lives, the emotional pain we experience makes it difficult to attend to ourselves. And yet, that is all we have to offer, our most well taken care of mind and body.

This space that we create is not to be confused with neglect, abandonment, self-centeredness, or indifference. A healthy parent, as opposed to a consumed parent, has more to offer: more boundaries, more emotional stability and calmness, more mental clarity and problem-solving ability, more receptivity, and more of an opportunity for joy, even in the midst of pain. From this position, life can be more than the stressors even when the stressors are immense.

Not unlike many other endeavors in life, gaining awareness becomes the first step on the path to change. Knowledge about the deleterious effects of prolonged stress can serve as a motivator to re-route energy pathways. The connection between mind and body is quite amazing and is well documented throughout medical, psychological, and scientific literature. Building the capacity for body awareness and utilizing tools to help turn off the stress response are important steps in redirecting focus and energy. If our life consists only of the stressors, we will be emotionally exhausted and have so little to offer ourselves or our children.

For some parents, the frightening and preoccupying situations experienced with their children may make this writing seem unsubstantial or the goals seem unobtainable. This was my internal debate when writing this book. The specific kind of emotional trauma that parents endure when their children are suffering does not lend itself to a fix or a solution. However, gathering together any scraps of resources that offer a slight change in perspective, a subtle shift toward self-care, something meaningful to put in your control, a willingness to attend to the potential physiological and psychological consequences of prolonged stress can serve as protective factors for parents. The more protected and resilient a parent can become the more available and present that parent will be in situations that create heartbreak.

I have been referring to this parental perspective as a paradigm change. When caught in the throngs of anxiety, fear and frustration involving the well-being of our children, achieving this perspective can appear not only excruciatingly difficult but neglectful or ineffective. A paradigm change involves a different way of looking at things. A loving parent will do anything to help their child. Determining what *is* help, in these most agonizing emotional situations, may be contradictory to a parent's natural inclinations.

A child, of any age, whose parents are practiced in self-regulating and self-protecting skills, has a most valuable resource available. Those parents are more likely to withstand the challenging emotional storms that may occur and be able to look toward a life beyond the stressors.

Glossary

Allostasis—the process of achieving stability through physiological or behavioral change (Wikipedia)

Allostatic load—the damage to the body when the individual is exposed to chronic stress (Wikipedia)

Amygdala—an almond shaped mass of gray matter in the front of the temporal lobe of the cerebrum that is involved in the processing of emotion

Adrenaline—a substance released in the body which causes the heart to beat faster and provides more energy during elevated emotions (Merriam-Webster)

Catecholamines—naturally occurring substances that function as neurotransmitters and hormones within the body

Cortisol—a steroid hormone that is released in response to stress

Endorphins—a group of hormones secreted within the brain and nervous system that activate the body's opiate receptors, cause an analgesic effect and can blunt pain

Glucocorticoids—steroid hormones that can reduce inflammation (Healthline)

Hippocampus—a small region of the brain that is part of the limbic system and primarily associated with memory and spatial navigation (News Medical)

HPA loop—the central stress response system involving the hypothalamic, pituitary, adrenal axis

Hypothalamus—a small section of the brain responsible for the production of many hormones. Its primary function is homeostasis (Healthline)

Parasympathetic Nervous System—the part of the nervous system that slows the heart rate and relaxes the muscles

Stress Response—also known as the fight-flight-freeze response

Sympathetic Nervous System—the part of the nervous system that increases heart rate, constricts blood vessels, and raises blood pressure

References

Abramson, Lyn Y. and Martin E. P. Seligman U. of Penn and John D. Teasdal, Oxford U. England Learned Helplessness in Humans: Critique and Reformulation. Journal of Abnormal Psychology 1978 Vol. 87 (49-59.

Ansell E.B., Rando, K., Tuit, K. Guarnaccia, J., Sinha, R. Cumulative adversity and smaller gray matter volume in medial prefrontal, anterior cingulate, and insula regions, Biol Psychiatry. 2012 Jul 1;72(1):57-64. doi: 10.1016/j.biopsych.2011.11.022. E-pub 2012 Jan 3.

Beck, Aaron, University of Pennsylvania - Aaron T. Beck, M.D. and Brad A. Alford, PhD Depression Causes and Treatment. Univ. of Pennsylvania Press Feb 2009.

Berkman Berkman, L. F. (1995). The role of social relations in health promotion. Psychosomatic Medicine, 57(3), 245-254.

Babyak, M.A., Blumenthal, J.A., Herman, S., Khatri, P., Doraiswamy, P.M., Moore, K.A. Craighead, W.E., Baldewicz, T.T., & Krishnan, K.R. "Exercise treatment for major depression: Maintenance of therapeutic benefit at 10 months." Psychosomatic Medicine, Vol. 63, 633-638.

Blumenthal, J.A., Babyak, M.A., Moore, K.A., Craighead, W.E., Herman, S., Khatri, P., Waugh, R., Napolitano, M.A., Forman, L.M., Appelbaum, M. Doraiswamy, P.M., & Krishman, K.R. "Effects of exercise training on older patients with major depression." Archives of Internal Medicine, Vol. 159, 2349-2356.

Brach Tara, "What keeps us from joy." Huffington Post, Aug. 15, 2013.

Brach, Tara, Radical Acceptance: Embracing Your Life With the Heart of a Buddha, Nov. 23, 2004.

Bredar, J. (Producer) (2008). Stress: Portrait of a killer [Television series episode]. In Bredar, J. (Executive Producer), National Geographic Special. National Geographic Television.

Bredar, J. (Producer) (2008). Stress: Portrait of a killer [Television series episode]. In Bredar, J. (Executive Producer), National Geographic Special. National Geographic Television.

Bredar, J. (Producer) (2008). Stress: Portrait of a killer [Television series episode]. In Bredar, J. (Executive Producer), National Geographic Special. National Geographic Television.

Cohen Sheldon and Syme Leonard Social Support and Health,. Eds. Academic Press, Orlando, Fla. 1985, xviii

Creswell, David, Michael Irwin, Lisa Burklund, Matthew Lieberman, Jesusa Arevalo, Jeffrey Ma, Elizabeth Breen, and Steven Cole. "Mindfulness-based Stress Reduction training reduces loneliness and pro-inflammatory gene expression in older adults: A small randomized controlled trial." Brain, Behavior, and Immunity. 26.7 (2012): 1095-1101. Print.

Epel, E. Profiles in Behavioral Science: the Science of Being Human, NIHOD YouTube video, Nov.27, 2012

Epel, E. Profiles in Behavioral Science Series, November 26,2012b

Fine, Sean 2013, HBO documentary film, http://www.hbo.com/documentaries/life-according-Sam.

Fleming, R., Baum, A., Gisriel, M. M., & Gatchel, R. (1982). Mediating influences of social support on stress at three mile island. Journal of Human Stress, 8(3), 14-22.

Geary, D. and Mark V. Flinn, Sex differences in behaviorial and hormonal response to socia threat: Commentary on Taylor et all (2000). American Psychological Assiciation 109 (4), 745.

Germer, CHristopher, Ronald Siegel, and Paul Fulton. Mindfulness and Psychotherapy. 1st edition. New York: The Gilford Press, 2005. Print.

Greenwood, B. N., Foley, T. E., Day, H. E. W., Campisi, J., Hammack, S. H., Campeau, S., Maier, S. F., & Fleshner, M. (2003). Freewheel running prevents learned helplessness/behavioral depression: Role of dorsal raphe serotonergic neurons. Journal of Neuroscience, 23(7), 2889-2898.

Hanson, Rick. Buddha's Brain: the practical neuroscience of happiness, love, and wisdom. (pp. 85). Oakland: New Harbinger Publications Inc, 2009. Print. (with Richard Mendius)

Harper, M "Increased Mortality Rates in parents bereaved in the first year of their child's life." BMJ Support Palliative Care 2011;1:306-309 doi:10.1136/bmjspcare-2011-000025

Hirota, Donald S. Locus of control and learned helplessness. Journal of Experiemental Psychology, Vol. 102(2), Feb 1974, 187-193

Hofmann, S., Sawyer, A., Witt, A., & Oh, D. (2010). Effects of mindfulness-based therapy on anxiety and depression: A meta-analytic review. Journal of Consulting and Clinical Psychology, 78(2), 169-183.

Hofmann, S.G., A.T. Sawyer, A.A. Witt, and D. Oh. "The Effect of mindfulness-based therapy on anxiety and depression: A meta-analytic review." Journal of Counseling and Clinical Psychology. 78.2 (2010): 169-183. Print.

House, J.S. Landis, KR, Umberson, D. Science 29, July 1088 Vol. 241 no 4865 pp. 540-545

Hozel, B. K., Carmody, J., Evans, K. C., Hoge, E. A., Dusek, J. A., Morgan, L., Pitman, R. K., & Lazar, S. W. (2010). Stress reduction correlates with structural changes in the amygdala. Social Cognitive and Affective Neuroscience, 5(1), 11-17.

Hurley, C. and Epel, E –TEDMED 2011, Jan. 30, 2012.

Institute for Learning and Brain Sciences; University of Washington

Kabat-Zinn, J. (1990a). Full catastrophe living. (p. 3). New York: Random House.

Kabat-Zinn, J. (2012a). Mindfulness for beginners. Boulder, CO: Sounds True Inc.

Kabat-Zinn, J. (2012b). Mindfulness for beginners. Boulder, CO: Sounds True Inc.

Kabat-Zinn, J. (2012c). Mindfulness for beginners. (pp. 2) Boulder, CO: Sounds True Inc.

Knauth, P. (1975). A season in hell. New York, NY: Harper and Row.

Leval, I., Friedlander, Y., Kark, J. D., & Peritz, E. (1988). An epidemiologic study of mortality among bereaved parents. New England Journal of Medicine, 319(8), 166.

Maguire, E. Navigation-related structural change in the hippocampi of taxi Cab Drivers. BBC News, Science/Nature, March 14, 2000, 15:51 GMT.

McEwen, B. (2002). The end of stress as we know it. Washington, DC: Joseph Henry Press.

Mindful magazine Dec 2013; Halifax, Nova Scotia, Canada B3J 1V7

Nataraja, Shanida. The Blissful Brain: Neuroscience and proof of the power of meditation. London: Octopus Publishing Group Ltd, 2008. Print.

Nataraja, Shanida. The Blissful Brain: Neuroscience and proof of the power of meditation. London: Octopus Publishing Group Ltd, 2008. Print.

Norman, J., White, W., and Pearce, D., "New possibilities in analgesia: the demand analgesia computer. Round table on morphinomimetics," 5th European Congress of Anesthesiology

O'Donohue, John Anam Cara, A Book of Celtic Wisdom, 1997, HarperCollins publishers, pg.102

Ratey, J. (2008a). Spark: The revolutionary new science of exercise and the brain. (p. 77). New York, NY: Little, Brown and Company.

Ratey, J. (2008b). Spark: The revolutionary new science of exercise and the brain. (p. 75). New York, NY: Little, Brown and Company.

Ratey, J. (2008c). Spark: The revolutionary new science of exercise and the brain. (p. 92). New York, NY: Little, Brown and Company.

Ratey, J. (2008d). Spark: The revolutionary new science of exercise and the brain. (p. 79). New York, NY: Little, Brown and Company.

Ratey, J. (2008e). Spark: The revolutionary new science of exercise and the brain. (p. ??). New York, NY: Little, Brown and Company.

Reynolds, Gretchen. New York Times.com, 2009 Phys Ed: Why Exercise Makes You Less Anxious, well. Blogs.

Sapolsky, R. (1994a). Why zebras don't get ulcers. (3rd ed.p.10). New York, NY: St Martin's Press.

Sapolsky, R. (1994b). Why zebra's don't get ulcers. (3rd ed., p. 396). New York, NY: St. Martin's Press.

Sapolsky, R. (1994c). Why zebra's don't get ulcers. (3rd ed., p. 396). New York, NY: St. Martin's Press.

Sapolsky, R. (1994d). Why zebra's don't get ulcers. (3rd ed., p. 275). New York, NY: St. Martin's Press.

Sapolsky, R. (1994e). Why zebra's don't get ulcers. (3rd ed., p. 305). New York, NY: St. Martin's Press

Sapolsky, R. (1994f). Why zebra's don't get ulcers. (3rd ed., p. 164). New York, NY: St. Martin's Press.

Sapolsky, R. (1994g). Why zebra's don't get ulcers. (3rd ed., p. 418). New York, NY: St. Martin's Press

Schneider, Robert H. et all "Long-term effects of stress reduction on mortality in persons-55years of age with systemic hypertension." The American Journal of cardiology 95.9 (2005): 1060-1064.)

Segal, Z., Williams, M., & Teasdale, J. (2002). Mindfulness-based cognitive therapy for depression. (p. viii). New York, NY: Guilford Publications Inc.

Seligman 1967 - reference needed

Selye, H. Stress in Health and Disease, New York, McGraw-Hill, 1976

Siegel, D. (2010a). Mindsight. (pp. 17-18). New York, NY: Random House Inc.

Siegel, D. (2010b). Mindsight. (pp. 18). New York, NY: Random House Inc.

Siegel, D. (2010c). Mindsight. (pp. 305). New York, NY: Random House Inc.

Siegel, D. (2010c). Mindsight. (pp. 305). New York, NY: Random House Inc.

Siegel, D. (2010d). Mindsight. (pp. 83). New York, NY: Random House Inc.

Siegel, D. (2010e). Mindsight. (pp. 85). New York, NY: Random House Inc.

Siegel, D. (2010f). Mindsight. (pp. 71). New York, NY: Random House Inc.

Siegel, D. (2010g). Mindsight. (pp. 18). New York, NY: Random House Inc.

Siegel, D. (2010h). Mindsight. (pp. 137). New York, NY: Random House Inc.

Singer, T.et all (2004). Empathy for pain involves the affective but not sensory components of pain. Science, 303 (5661), 1157-1162.

Solomon, M., & Tatkin, S. (2011a). Love and war in intimate relationships. New York, NY: W.W. Norton & Co.

Solomon, M., & Tatkin, S. (2011b). Love and war in intimate relationships. (p. 210) New York, NY: W.W. Norton & Co.

Stranahan, Alexis, David Khalil, and Elizabeth Gould. "Social Isolation delays the positive effects of running on adult neurogenesis." Nature Neuroscience. 9. 526-533. Print.

Taylor, S. E., Klein, L. C., Lewis, B. P., Gruenewald, T. L., Gurung, R. A. R., & Updegraff, J. A. (2000). Biobehavioral responses to stress in females: Tend-and-befriend, not fight-or-flight. Psychological Review, 107(3), 411-29.

Turner-Cobb,, J, Sephton, S, Koopman,, C, Blake-Mortimer, J, and Spiegal, D, 2000

Twyman, Richard; Social Support and Salivary Cortisol in Women with Metastic Breast Cancer, Psychosom Med. 2000 May-June (3): 337-45.

Wall Street Journal, March 22, 2014

Watson, J. (2013, January 19). Marines studying mindfulness-based training. The Seattle Times. Retrieved from http://http://seattletimes.com/html/nationworld/2020170038_apusmeditatingmarines.html

White WD, Pearce DJ, Norman J. Postoperative analgesia: a comparison of intravenous on-demand fentanyl with epidural bupivacaine. *Br Med J.* 1979 Jul 21;2(6183):166–167.

Zeidan, F., S.K. Johnson, B.J. Diamond, Z. David, and P. Goolkasian. "Mindfulness meditation improves cognition: Evidence of brief mental training." Conciousness and cognition. 19.2 (2010): 597-605. Print.